D0485350

CAN WE HAVE ONE?

CAN WE HAVE ONE?

A PARENT'S GUIDE TO RAISING
KIDS WITH CATS AND DOGS

Lynn F. Buzhardt, DVM, and

Sue D. Steib, MSW, PhD

LOUISIANA STATE UNIVERSITY PRESS
Baton Rouge

)|(

Northern Plains Public Library
Ault Colorado

Published by Louisiana State University Press
Copyright © 2008 by Louisiana State University Press
All rights reserved
Manufactured in the United States of America

An LSU Press Paperback Original
FIRST PRINTING

DESIGNER: *Amanda McDonald Scallan*
TYPEFACE: *Whitman, Will, and Scala Sans*
PRINTER AND BINDER: *Thomson-Shore, Inc.*

Library of Congress Cataloging-in-Publication Data

Buzhardt, Lynn F.
  Can we have one? : a parent's guide to raising kids with cats
and dogs / Lynn F. Buzhardt, Sue D. Steib.
    p. cm.
  Includes bibliographical references and index.
  ISBN 978-0-8071-3377-4 (pbk. : alk. paper)
  1. Pets. 2. Children and animals. 3. Human-animal
relationships. I. Steib, Sue D. II. Title.
  SF411.5B89 2005
  636.088'7—dc22
                                        2008014735
The paper in this book meets the guidelines for permanence
and durability of the Committee on Production Guidelines
for Book Longevity of the Council on Library Resources. ∞

Contents

Note to Readers

This book is intended to inform parents and parents-to-be about the major issues involved in blending pets, particularly dogs and cats, into a household with children. It is not a substitute for direct behavioral or medical consultation or treatment for either animals or children. Indeed, much of the guidance offered here is intended to make parents better informed consumers of such services.

CAN WE HAVE ONE?

Photo by Linell Champagne

Introduction

What parent hasn't heard the plea: "Mom, Dad, let's get a pet, please. Please can we have one? Please!" This book is designed to help parents decide how to respond to this entreaty—and to know what to do if the answer is "yes." It's about the many things a wise parent will consider before deciding to get an animal and about how to deal with situations that arise when a pet is part of the household.

The book also addresses the needs of parents of furry four-legged children who are about to have their first human child. Such parents need to address several issues before the two-legged child arrives.

Pet ownership can have many benefits for families, and particularly for children. But before introducing a pet into the home, parents need to think carefully about the demands that animals make and the family's ability to adequately meet those demands. In this book we offer information that will enable families to avoid situations that can contribute to pet-inflicted injuries and illnesses, injury or maltreatment of pets, or emotionally traumatic animal relinquishment.

Fortunately, most of the problems that bring heartache to pet-owning families can be eliminated or at least minimized with thoughtful planning and preparation. Our goal is to help people provide happy homes for pets while allowing children to receive the maximum benefit of the pet-child relationship and letting parents enjoy the balanced family unit such a relationship creates.

This book focuses on the acquisition and ownership of dogs and cats, although much of it is applicable to other animals as well. We do not, however, provide detailed information about the selection and care of small caged mammals, reptiles, and amphibians, or of other exotic pets. We limit our attention to dog and cat ownership for several reasons: (1) Dogs and cats are the most common pets in American households.[1] (2) The limited research on the human-animal bond suggests that these animals are the pets to which both children and adults in Western culture are most likely to form the strongest attachments.[2] (3) Largely because of the prevalence of dogs and cats as household pets, they are most often the subject of parents' animal-related child safety and health concerns. (4) These are the animals that are at greatest risk for relinquishment to shelters.[3]

Pets ask a lot from their owners, but they give much more in return. We draw on the emerging scientific evidence and our professional knowledge and experience to address the social, emotional, educational, and developmental benefits that children may derive from sharing their lives with animals. And we offer ways in which parents can maximize those benefits. Parents, too, may turn to the family pet for a much-needed dose of unconditional support and affection.

Our concern is for animals as well. Every year in the United States, millions of animals are relinquished to shelters. Because shelters are not required to report their intake and disposition of animals, exact numbers are unknown. In a 1997 survey conducted by the National Council on Pet Population Study and Policy (NCPPSP), one thousand of an estimated thirty-five hundred shelters in the United States reported admitting a total of 4.3 million animals, of which 2.7 million were euthanized.[4] Another NCPPSP study found that families moving, landlord issues, and cost of maintenance were among the top five reasons for relinquishing a dog or cat.[5] A 2002 survey of people who had adopted pets found that the animals were more likely to be relinquished when they had been acquired specifically for a child or grandchild.[6] These findings suggest that better planning and preparation can prevent both the tragic loss of animal life and the human pain associated with relinquishing a family pet.

This book is only one source of information available on pet behavior, the safety of children with pets, and pet-related child-health concerns. Indeed, parents may spend countless hours reviewing Internet sites, magazine articles, and a wealth of books on various aspects of pet care and selection as well as the medical and developmental benefits and risks of pet-child relationships.

Photo by Linell Champagne

What sets this book apart is its all-in-one approach on how to establish a household that safely and successfully integrates children, cats, and dogs. We have gathered the most critical information into a single resource, backed it up with medical and social science research data, and organized it in a volume designed specifically for busy parents. We raise the common issues related to family pet ownership and offer recommendations that are straightforward, practical, easy to understand, and easily implemented. Each chapter concludes with a brief summary of points to remember and a checklist of to-do items.

Positive and satisfying experiences for families and pets can be achieved when parents understand the important issues in pet selection and care, know how to manage interaction between children and pets, and can guard against pet-related child injury and illness. This book provides parents with the information necessary to make wise decisions about how to create a blended family that's made up of kids and pets.

Whether you are bringing a baby into a home that includes pets or adding pets to an existing family, the message of this book is stop, think, and prepare. Yes, spontaneity can be fun, but pet ownership, especially when children are involved, is too serious a business to be undertaken impulsively.

If you already own a pet and are looking forward to the birth of your first child, carefully evaluate your pet as well as your own expectations and begin immediately to give the animal the preparation it will need to accept the new member of your family. The steps we outline in chapter 1 require some effort, but all are doable and will go a long way toward creating greater harmony in your home and ensuring the baby's safety when he or she arrives.

For many families, the question of pet ownership arises after the first child comes along. Parents may feel the need to have a pet "for the child." And in Western cultures, most children, at one time or another, indicate a desire for a pet. But parents must be the ones to determine whether the family's circumstances will allow them to act on their own desire or the child's to include a pet in the family.

Adding pets to a household with children calls for careful timing, prudent selection, consistent supervision, and attention to how both you and your children interact with your companion animals. It also means, at some point, dealing head-on with the pain of loss and then undertaking the same careful scrutiny when you consider sharing your life with another animal.

Like all aspects of parenting, successfully integrating children and pets can be challenging, but pets can bring greater warmth, laughter, and joy to families as they teach children important lessons about kindness, selflessness, loyalty, and responsibility. Pets can be a wonderful, meaningful part of family life. What a joy it is to watch your children grow up with a pet they love. We hope that the lessons offered here will contribute to greater happiness for you and all the members of your family, those with four feet as well as two.

Photo by Linell Champagne

Photo by Linell Champagne

CHAPTER 1

AND BABY MAKES FOUR

Bringing a Baby into a Pet-Owning Household

THE ROLE OF PETS IN DELAYED PARENTHOOD

The picture of the traditional family has changed over the decades. Unlike the 1950s stereotypes, Mom may not bake cookies while supervising the children as they do their homework. Dad may not lounge in the den smoking his pipe and reading the newspaper. Children may not spend the afternoon in the tree house reading a book. Moms and dads have definitely evolved and even the "child" component of American families is different. In fact, the American family has gone to the dogs . . . and to the cats.

Pets have assumed an important role in the family structure, especially in those families that don't yet have children. The old skipping rhyme "First comes love, then comes marriage, then comes Susie with a baby carriage" does not now necessarily reflect the order of events. Many couples find love and even marry, but the baby carriage may remain in the store window.

Adults delay parenthood for various reasons. Perhaps they aren't ready to accept the confines and obligations of parenting. Perhaps they want to reach a targeted degree of financial independence before having a child. Or maybe they recognize the medical advances that allow women to safely conceive and bear a child at an older age, so they don't hear the biological clock ticking quite as loudly as in the past. Whatever the reason, many couples decide to wait a while before having their first baby.

But do they need something in the childless interim? Is living as a couple enough? Are people happy when the only thing they nurture is an adult relationship? The answer varies, of course, but many couples recognize that shared nurturing adds another dimension to an existing relationship. And dogs and cats are happy to play their part in bringing human relationships to another level. So, in many households the first addition to the family will have four feet, fur, and a wet tongue that doles out licks as kisses.

Couples derive countless benefits from owning a pet. For starters, pets help organize our lives. Having a pet in the household establishes a routine. Humans *have* to be present to provide the basic essentials of life for the pet, so household schedules often center on pet care. Pets can't fix their own dinner or bathe themselves or even relieve themselves properly without a little human assistance. Someone has to change that litter box or open the back door. This routine adds stability and a level of domestic comfort to the home.

In essence, dogs and cats are children that never grow up—at least not enough to be fully independent. They always need us, which can be a wonderful feeling. And they love us no matter what. When we share that love (along with the responsibilities for pet care) with our mate, we strengthen our relationship with the pet and with each other. Taking care of a pet is a joint effort, but we don't just share the work; we share the fun. To fully appreciate this concept, just watch a couple as they describe their pet's antics with a shared sense of love and pride. Or smile as a proud pet owner reaches into his wallet to show off a photo of his dog or cat.

ADDING A CHILD TO THE FAMILY

Living as a family that dotes on its furry, four-legged members is great, but what happens when the time comes to have a baby? What happens to the existing family unit of Mom, Dad, and Fluffy? From the pet's perspective, the family unit is a "pack," the traditional family unit in the wild. This particular pack includes humans, but the pet understands its position in that pack. It understands that Mom and Dad are the alpha members (or should be) and that it has the role of dutiful child.

In the pet's eyes, the family unit is in perfect balance. Adding a baby is likely to change the family dynamics—not necessarily for the better. When a new baby comes into the home, every family member is affected. Granted, the dog or cat won't wake up in the middle of the night to feed the baby and won't have diaper duty, but the pet's life is affected all the same.

There are many things to do before having a baby. If you have a household pet, you need to add one more duty to the preparenting list. Early preparation of the existing family unit will minimize the disruption of the prebaby pack, making life much easier for the frazzled new parents, less threatening for the pet, and safer for the baby.

Future parents can't start too soon in readying the pet for the "infant intruder." This scary little being smells funny, makes terrifying sounds, and steals parental attention. The new baby is a potential threat to even the most self-confident cat or dog. So when you learn that a baby is on the way, celebrate, call all the appropriate friends and relatives, and then get to work preparing the household for the arrival of the new baby.

Early preparation is key to an easy transition in the household, and it requires some effort. Unfortunately, the months during pregnancy are usually quite busy. All parents-to-be have work to do as they prepare for their new baby. Those with dogs or cats just have a little more work to do. Expectant parents shop for the safest car seat and the best baby bed and read the most informative books on child care. Families with pets simply add another task to the list: preparing the first child to meet the second child. In other words, teaching the pet to accept the baby before the baby is ever born.

Your pet is accustomed to being the focal point of your family. He expects you to spend lots of time with him and you probably do—now. Since free time is a rare commodity after the birth of a baby, help your pet adjust to spending less one-on-one time with you. Encourage him to play alone by providing new toys, and encourage him to rest quietly, too. Newborns require so much time from parents that your pet may feel a little neglected at first. Help him adjust to the new time schedule now.

BACK TO SCHOOL

Even the smartest dogs need a refresher course in obedience occasionally. And if your dog has never been to obedience school, now is the time. Sign up for the next available course. Much of the work you do preparing your dog for the baby's arrival depends on his ability to follow your commands. It's difficult to desensitize a dog to the changes associated with babyhood if he never learned the difference between positive and negative reinforcement. That's like trying to correct a child who doesn't understand the difference between the words "yes" and "no."

Well-behaved dogs should respond to voice commands alone; though new parents may wish for more hands, they still have only one pair. As you enter the back door with the baby in one arm and a diaper bag on the other, you cannot tug on the dog's leash as he tries to jump into your arms. You cannot physically give a "down" command when both hands are full. And who wants to drop the baby to still the dog?

To avoid unnecessary "baby juggling," you must be assured that your dog will respond to the basic voice commands of "sit," "stay," and "down." For example, as you enter the back door and the dog jumps on you in greeting, give the "down" command. If you are feeding the baby and the dog is nervously dancing in front of the rocking chair, how about a firm command of "sit"? When you are making a mad dash to the changing table with a leaky diaper that's still attached to the baby, wouldn't it be nice to simply use the "stay" word?

Voice commands are also handy when you want your dog to rest nearby as you tend to the baby. How cozy it is to have your pet near you as you feed the baby . . . just not *too* close. If your pet is accustomed to jumping in your lap which is already occupied by the baby, wouldn't it be nice to utter "down" and have him actually obey? Then when the time is right for you to invite your dog to join you on the couch, ask him to "come" or say "here" or "up."

Obedience classes will help the dog learn how to respond to voice commands. If Fido is already a graduate, you may want to go for a refresher course. Classes also allow you to spend more quality time with your dog before the baby arrives. And you'll never regret the time you spent in prebaby canine education during postbaby crunch times.

EXPOSING THE PET TO ENVIRONMENTAL CHANGES

Preparing the dog or cat for the infant's arrival doesn't have to be a daunting task if the preparation is taken in stages. Don't overload the pet or yourself. Keep it simple. Take your time while helping the pet adjust to the imminent changes that will occur in his environment once Junior arrives. Remember that pets rely on their senses to understand their environment. They need to be accustomed to the sights, sounds, and smells associated with infants.

A Sight for Sore Eyes

Many changes must occur in a household in order to accommodate the baby. Babies come with a caravan of infant paraphernalia. The key is to add these items to the household early in the pregnancy so that the pet has time to grow accustomed to them. Don't wait until the last minute to buy the crib or bassinet. Set up the nursery two or three months before your due date and allow the dog or cat to explore the new contraptions that now take up space in his once orderly environment. The pet's initial fascination will usually turn to disinterest. After all, how interesting can a changing table be?

The nursery isn't the only room of the house that will change. The entire house will reflect the new family addition, so expose your pet to other infant-care items, too. Baby walkers, swings, baby bottles, and new toys can upset the pet's sense of normalcy. A lowly diaper bag can fascinate or frighten even the brightest, most worldly pet.

Don't confine the baby items just to the nursery. Place these items in different areas of the house where they may be used. Put the swing in the family room if you think you will use it there. The pet will get the message that the entire household is undergoing an adjustment and so is he.

You'll also need to give some attention to baby items used outside the home. Place the car seat and diaper bag in the car and take the pet for a ride. If the baby seat is going to be located in the dog's usual car spot, relocate the traveling pet now. Get him accustomed to his new position in the car by rewarding him for acceptance.

If you walk your dog and intend to include the baby on your outdoor jaunts, now is the time to introduce the baby stroller. What an odd looking contraption to a dog. What interesting turning wheels to chase. No matter how silly you feel, you should walk your dog alongside an empty stroller to get him accustomed to this moving device and to show him the proper way to walk beside it.

If you and your spouse routinely walk the dog together, you may want to take turns walking him alone. Immediately after the baby is born, Mom may not be up to a walk, so the dog needs to learn that walking with one parent is OK. Also, there will be times when one of you may need to be home with the sleeping, hungry, or grouchy baby while the other (lucky) one walks the dog.

Even though many baby dolls are lifelike, they are not the real thing. Nonetheless, having a baby doll in the house may help your dog become accustomed to a smaller human being. Swaddle the doll and carry it around the house, put it in the baby seat, and take it for a walk in the stroller—all in the presence of the dog or cat.

While introducing your pet to all these impending changes, reward her for appropriate behavior (curiosity) and reprimand her for an inappropriate response (vandalization). Praise and correction are both important in helping the pet adjust to the new household arrangements. A word of praise to the dog or cat that investigates new items and moves on is a good idea. Likewise, a verbal reprimand is necessary for the pet that scratches, chews, or sprays the new item.

Positive reinforcement usually helps pets accept the new household items, reducing the amount of correction needed. Hopefully, the dog or cat will accept these additions as part of the regular scheme of things by the time the baby arrives.

Name That Tune

The entire character of a household changes when a baby arrives. A lot of these changes are auditory.

Face it; all babies cry and that sound can often frighten even the parents. Imagine how a screaming baby can disturb a pet, which has a more acute sense of hearing than any person. Pets must be desensitized to the crying infant before they come face to face with the actual source of the noise. This tedious process should prevent harmful behavior that may arise out of a pet's sense of fear or protectiveness when he hears the crying infant.

Cats usually respond to a crying infant by simply removing themselves from the noxious noise. Rarely will a cat do more than simply approach a vocalizing infant. They just don't like to be disturbed, so they find a quiet spot elsewhere in the house.

Dogs are different. They have been known to respond to a crying infant by vocalizing themselves, which only adds to the pandemonium. Others become agitated and prance around nervously. Still others become so agitated that they approach the source of the noise and try through inappropriate means to make it stop.

It's easy to see how dog bites can be provoked by crying babies. The dog may be fearful of the noise, feel that it's being attacked, and respond aggressively. On the other hand, some dogs feel quite protective of the newest member of the pack and will alert the leader of the pack to the infant's obvious distress signal. Both responses can mean danger to the infant. Well-intentioned large dogs have been known to actually pick the baby up from the bassinet and "carry" him to the parent for assistance. It's not difficult to see how injury can result from this protective behavior.

That's why it's important that dogs and cats understand that infant crying is a normal, acceptable household sound. They need to learn that a crying baby doesn't mean that there is a household emergency and doesn't pose a threat to anyone's safety. The noise is just a new part of daily life with a baby.

To desensitize the dog to this disturbing sound, pet owners should introduce the dog to the sound in a controlled, comfortable, safe environment. Of course, it's hard to produce a crying infant every time a parent has time for dog training, so having a recording of a crying infant provides a readily available sound source. You may tape the sound from television, Internet sources, or ask friends or relatives to tape their baby's cries. Assure them that the request is made from the noblest of intentions.

Another solution is to purchase a CD of baby sounds. Created by two mothers, Lisa Ruggles and Shawn Hrncir, "Preparing Fido" is filled not only with unhappy baby sounds like crying but also happy ones like cooing and giggling.[1]

Desensitization takes time and should be accomplished incrementally. Start by playing the recording at a low volume during a calm part of the day with the pet fully relaxed. Pet and comfort the dog or cat while listening to the tape. Kind words should assure the pet that this sound is "OK." If the pet becomes too agitated by the noise, render even more assurance with words and petting to calm him. Once he does calm down, offer praise for good behavior.

If the pet becomes aggressive, reprimand him appropriately and turn off the recording. Calm the pet, then turn on the recording again. Repeat the process until the pet no longer growls or assumes a dominant posture, then reward the good behavior. If the pet isn't aggressive but becomes too agitated and upset and cannot be calmed, turn the recording off and try again at a later time. After the pet becomes accustomed to the crying noise at a low volume, begin increasing the volume.

Next, play the recording during different times of the day and night. Pets need to become accustomed to having their sleep interrupted, so expose the pet to the crying baby noise during nap time. Also, turn on the recorder during dinnertime, early morning busy time, when guests are present, and during playtime. The pet needs to learn that a crying infant cannot tell time.

Play the tape in different parts of the house, yard, and even in the car. In other words, play the recording anytime and anywhere you can imagine the baby's crying. This teaches the pet to accept the sound in various environments, during different levels of activity, at all different times of the day or night. Babies don't cry all the time—they coo and giggle, making the sweetest sounds in the world. Your dog or cat needs to hear these too.

Offering treats may help facilitate acceptance of the sound but may also create a level of canine expectation that new parents simply can't fulfill. It's not easy to grab a dog biscuit every time the baby cries. This pattern of behavior modification could result in harried parents and obese dogs. Most dogs respond to positive verbal reinforcement of good behavior, so praise is usually all the reward they need. And even parents who have both hands occupied with a screaming infant can manage a word of praise.

Don't forget the other sounds that come along with an infant. The sound of an automatic diaper disposal may raise a few canine and feline eyebrows. And what about the sound of the automatic swing or the vibrating baby seat? These can be disturbing too. And then there will be music—from the mobile, from baby tapes, and even from you. Turn on the music and sing to your pet. Your singing may be the scariest sound of all and the pet will need ample time to adjust.

Where's That Smell Coming From?

Babies smell sooo good, just not all the time. There are some things that even the best parents don't appreciate about their babies, and dirty diapers top the list.

Parental responses to drippy, smelly diapers range from repulsion to tolerance. Changing diapers is a necessary task that parents undertake because they love their child. Dogs, on the other hand, may view that soiled diaper a bit differently. While some dogs are put off by the smell, others relish it.

THE DIAPER DILEMMA

Dogs may sense undigested milk products or baby food in the diaper and hate to see "good food" go to waste. Many dismayed parents have walked into the nursery to find their well-fed dog hovering over a toppled diaper pail enjoying the treasures inside like he has never had a good meal.

Although it is a disgusting sight, the dog is usually unharmed by his dietary indiscretion. Some dogs may have a bout of diarrhea after diaper dining because they cannot digest the sugars in certain milk products. Fortunately, these are usually self-resolving symptoms; however, persistent gastrointestinal upsets should be reported to the veterinarian.

Now, how do you avoid the diaper dilemma? Innovations such as diaper disposals have certainly reduced the dog's access to this delicacy. But dogs are quick

Photo by Lynn Buzhardt

to snatch the treat before it can reach the disposal. So desensitization to the smell of a baby's eliminations is important.

This requires making another request of baby-owning friends by conscientious parents-to-be, and it's worse than asking them to record their baby's cries—you need to ask for a wet or soiled diaper. They may think you're crazy, but it will be worth the embarrassment in the long run.

Dirty diaper in hand, allow your dog or cat to smell the offending object. Cats will usually defer and in typical feline fashion, simply walk away. Dogs are a bit more curious. Allow the dog a good whiff, but if he tries to take the diaper out of your hand or tries to mouth it, reprimand him. As usual, reward good responses with praise. Later, if possible, you should bring home a diaper from your own newborn while he is still in the hospital. It is also a good idea to bring home a piece of clothing that the baby has worn in the hospital to expose the pet to additional odors associated with your particular infant.

SWEET BABY SMELLS: LOTIONS, POWDERS, ETC.

Not all baby aromas are offensive. Some are quite pleasant. The smell of baby powder and lotion evokes warm feelings in many adults. They may, however, spell trouble if the dog only associates them with the intruder to the pack. When doing visual training with the lifelike baby doll, you can apply a little baby powder or lotion to the doll to give the pet a whiff of things to come. Parents should also expose the pet to these smells when they are associated with an already-accepted family member—themselves.

Future moms and dads should rub baby powder and lotion on their own hands and then interact with the dog or cat. Pets are more likely to accept this aroma when it's presented by a trusted friend. Then when they smell the same scent on the new baby, it has a positive association.

Other infant aromas to introduce include baby wipes and detergents. Introduce a freshly laundered baby blanket to your pet and see how it responds. And bring out an unused diaper (cloth or disposable). Pets need to smell clean diapers, too. The basic reward/reprimand reenforcement should be implemented here.

Introduce baby wipes in the same manner. Baby wipes are envied objects for both cats and dogs. They smell different *and* their containers make good chew toys. Oh, boy! Two treats in one. However, swallowing baby wipes is no joke. These fiber wipes aren't very digestible and can cause serious obstruction in the pet's gastro-intestinal tract. If your pet swallows a baby wipe, notify your veterinarian at once.

Remember to continue exposing the pet to new baby smells that may come into play. If the infant needs a new diaper cream or medicinal ointment, allow the pet to sniff it and follow the usual behavior modification techniques.

AHH . . . DESSERT: BABY FOOD AND FORMULA

Pets should also be introduced to the smell of baby food and formula. Some dogs will eat just about anything, but even finicky cats are tempted to partake of baby food or milk and must be taught that it's off-limits.

Keeping baby bottles away from feline paws is harder than keeping them out of canine clutches because parents can place them on counters out of the dog's reach. But cats can, and often do, climb anywhere. Scaling a mere kitchen cabinet for a delicacy is nothing for a cat in search of a snack, and bottles dropped on the floor by babies give even the shortest-legged dog easy access to a new treat.

Desensitization of dogs to baby food and milk entails the same steps as behavior modification for sights, sounds, and other smells. Exposure with appropriate parental response to positive or negative behavior of the dog will usually prevent your pet from having an impromptu snack.

Desensitizing cats may require a special tactic. Some cats will respond to verbal reprimands, but others simply ignore them. Here's the feline approach. Allow the cat access to the bottle or baby food. Let him smell it and investigate it. If the cat proceeds to partake, approach three of his senses—sight, sound, and touch. Let him hear and see that you are serious by the tone of your voice and facial expression as you reprimand him, much as when you reprimand a dog. In addition, let him feel the result of the infraction by either squirting a water pistol or physically removing him from the tempting treat. Repeat this process, ending with praise for positive responses.

Only through consistent parental responses to canine and feline misbehavior are lessons learned, so both parents need to be on the same page of the pet training book. And while the lessons are in progress, remember that baby bottles can be cleaned sufficiently to erase any evidence of "student" contact.

PLAY TIME! HOW TO DEAL WITH TOY-SHARING

Even the neatest parents will occasionally leave a few baby toys on the floor in plain sight and within easy reach of the pet. And often, pets even manage to reach toys that are left in "safe" places. Cats are particularly agile and can find access to almost every nook and cranny in a home, reducing the number of "safe" places dramatically. How concerned should parents be about the inevitable "sharing" of pet and baby toys?

While dogs and cats do harbor bacteria in their mouths, human oral cavities are not sterile either. Nonetheless, having your pet's teeth professionally cleaned on a regular basis is medically prudent, and you should follow your veterinarian's advice on home care to minimize oral bacteria. Even so, it is smart to avoid the sharing of toys and pacifiers as much as possible. Why tempt fate?

When the dog or cat does manage to pilfer the baby's toy, it's a good idea to clean the toy. Household detergents should remove any contamination. So you may want to shop for toys that are washable. Many cloth toys can be cleaned in the washing machine, and many plastic ones are dishwasher safe.

And let's not assume that dogs and cats are always the culprits. Dog and cat toys are often quite attractive to more mobile infants and toddlers. Curiosity often prevails as the child forsakes his own basketful of toys to snatch the dog's well-worn chew toy.

Toy-sharing poses three situations that must be addressed:

1. Teaching the dog or cat to stay away from baby toys.
2. Teaching the dog or cat to give up *any* toy, its or the baby's, without a fight.
3. Teaching the baby not to "steal" the pet's toys and how to respond if the pet "steals" one of her toys.

That's a lot of teaching.

Situation number one should have been addressed in the prebaby lessons, but here's the refresher course. Leave the baby's toys in full view of the pet and allow sufficient time for investigation. If the pet is simply not interested in the toys, the lesson is a short one. If the pet is mesmerized by the toys and chooses to further its investigation by claiming one with its mouth, render a gentle, but firm rebuke. Repeat the lesson as before with positive rewards when appropriate.

Lesson number two is a tricky one. When dogs manage to snatch up a toy seemingly abandoned on the floor or when they are playing with their own toy, parents should be able to remove it from the dog's mouth without provoking an aggressive response. If the dog snaps at the person taking the toy away, trouble is brewing. Dogs must relinquish *anything* in their mouths to *any human*, large or small, without biting.

Lesson number three requires teaching the child instead of the dog. Children with all the toys in the world will sometimes find the dog's favorite chew toy more interesting—often when the dog is actually chewing on it. And possessive toddlers *will* try to reclaim their "stolen" toys by tugging them from the dog's grasp. Babies tugging at any item in the dog's mouth are in a potentially dangerous situation.

You need to rely on prebaby behavior modifications to get the dog to relinquish the baby's toy or even *his own* most cherished toy without a fight. Your dog must understand verbal correction, but as soon as children are able to understand the most commonly used word, "NO!" they must be taught to respect the dog's space, too.

When children do begin to understand positive and negative reinforcement themselves, life becomes a little easier. Then children can learn an important lesson: The child should not steal the pet's toys and he should let the dog borrow his toys without a fight. Here's where the true art of sharing comes in. Toddlers should understand that the proper response to the dog stealing their toy is either no response at all or a loud call for Mom or Dad. The child should be taught that taking something out of the dog's mouth is not a good response to canine thievery.

Sharing toys has two possible consequences. The first is the exchange of oral bacteria, which usually does not pose a serious health issue for the child or the dog. The second is the potential for injury that can occur when either the child or the dog refuses to share. Proper education of the pet *and* the child should result in a happy ending to both story lines.

HOUSEHOLD BOUNDARIES: WHO GOES WHERE?

Making room for a new baby may challenge expectant parents. Designating a particular room as the nursery and setting aside additional areas in other rooms for baby items upsets the household floor plan. Imagine how upsetting this change in space can be for a dog or cat that views the house as the center of the entire universe?

Every expectant couple makes alterations in the household to accommodate a new baby. The key is to make these changes early in the pregnancy to allow time for pets and parents to adjust. This allows you to see how the household arrangement will work. It also helps you decide if your pet will have full or limited access to the house.

Let's start with the most important room, the nursery. Many parents are happy to allow the dog or cat into the nursery, while others are uncomfortable with this idea. They have nightmares remembering old wives' tales about cats snuffing out a baby's breath or fearing that the dog may contaminate a supposedly pristine area.

If the pet, canine or feline, will not be allowed in the baby's room or on the baby's bed, begin training right away to enforce the new limitations in household boundaries. A cat or dog that has had full run of a house will need time to adjust to newly imposed restrictions.

Cat Tales

Stories about cats stealing the baby's breath are just that, stories. But cats can and do lie down anywhere they choose, and if they choose to lie on an immobile infant's face, tragedy may result. For this reason, many parents call the baby's bed off-limits to the cat.

In addition, cat feet go from the litter pan to the baby's bed without being disinfected. And litter pans are loaded with bacteria and sometimes with parasites from fecal contamination. So in general, baby beds are better off being cat free.

Warning: Restricted Area

Although simply closing the door will keep cats and dogs out of the nursery, parents usually prefer not to have the baby in a closed-off room. An open door allows you to have a quick peek at your baby. To avoid having the door closed, you may consider setting up baby gates.

Baby gates set at a nursery's doorway work well to limit a dog's access, but they don't do much to keep out a cat. Cats can easily scale a baby gate, so some parents resort to more extreme measures such as doubling the baby gates hanging one low and another high to cover the open space. Others hang a screen door in the nursery entrance. Both of these options allow you visual and auditory access to the baby, but are sometimes annoying impediments. And with consistent behavior modification, neither obstacle should be necessary.

Back to Pet Training 101. Remember how you set up the nursery in advance of the baby's birth? Here's why. If the nursery will be entirely off-limits, first allow the pet to explore the room that will be beyond his reach in order to satisfy his curiosity. Then remove him from the nursery.

Later, bring the cat or dog to the threshold of the baby's room and dole out reprimands for intrusions, followed by rewards when the limits are respected. Eventually, most pets get the message.

But cats aren't most pets. They are known to be finicky, and canine logic doesn't always prevail in the feline psyche. Verbal reprimands alone often do not deter cats, which, unlike dogs, don't live for the sole purpose of pleasing their owners. But cats' very peculiarity aids in training them.

Cats dislike many things in this world, but a couple of the things they dislike the most are loud noises and water. Reprimanding the cat with the traditional loud "NO!" accompanied by a squirt from a water pistol may help in the training. Your cat will probably decide that crossing the threshold to the nursery simply isn't worth it.

If the cat does choose to breach the nursery door and head for the baby's bed, additional tricks may be used. One way to train the cat not to jump on the bed is to place tin pie plates closely together on the surface of the bed. When the cat jumps on the bed and lands on a plate, it snaps up, makes a noise, and pops the cat without causing him harm. If the cat manages to avoid the pie plate land mines when jumping on the bed, he will eventually walk on one of the plates with the same result.

If the cat successfully lands on the bed, does not step on a plate, and has the audacity to "mark" the bed, the urine spray splatters off the pie plate, making more noise and wetting the cat to boot, so the deterrence factor is doubled. Some people still like to use a water gun to reprimand the cat that invades forbidden turf or render a firm "NO!" accompanied with moving the cat from the bed, but this method requires constant monitoring, which may not be practical for busy couples. Pie plates are inexpensive, less time consuming, and usually work as well. Aluminum foil may also be effective.

Using double-stick tape on the baby bed is yet another option. Cats, and dogs too, are annoyed by the sticky sensation on their foot pads. A couple of words of warning with this technique: Test the tape on an inconspicuous area of the furniture first to make sure that the adhesive does not mar the wood. Also, check the tape frequently to make sure it's firmly adhered to the furniture. If your cat or dog ends up with a piece of tape on a paw and swallows it while trying to remove it, the consequences may be serious.

Frustrated owners of very stubborn cats have resorted to crib netting to keep the cat out of the baby bed. This is a viable option, but usually the desire for the cat to jump into the baby's bed can be curbed without such impediments.

While small dogs can't usually jump on baby beds like their feline friends, large dogs can easily stand on their hind legs and peer over the bed rails. Utilizing the usual deterrent methods should break this habit in short order.

Who's Allowed in the "Big Bed"?

Another bedroom situation that needs to be addressed involves the master bedroom. Many cats and dogs have access to the master bedroom and actually sleep in the owners' bed. But new parents may find the bed a bit crowded when the baby is added to the mix. They may also be reluctant to allow the pet in the same bed with the baby for health reasons.

Parents who do want to continue sharing the "big bed" with their pets should consider a few medical issues. First, the cat or dog should be free of fleas and ticks that can transmit diseases to humans and are just plain yucky. In addition, pets may have intestinal parasite infections that have a slight chance of contaminating the bedding and infecting humans. Note, the word is "slight." The problem of human-animal transmission of disease is covered in chapter 6, but common sense and good hygiene are helpful guides.

Normal laundering of bed linens should eliminate the possibility of harboring fleas, ticks, or intestinal parasites. Furthermore, if the dog and cat are given year-round parasite control medication, the risk of disease transmission is greatly reduced. But, there is still the "germ" factor associated with pets, and they will shed hair on the bed. So after considering these medical facts and assessing the spatial limitations of the bed itself, if you decide that the pet should stop sleeping in your bed, it is important to begin retraining the dog or cat as soon as you find out you are expecting.

Early alteration in household sleeping arrangements will avoid having the pet "blame the baby" for any changes that occur. The baby needs to arrive with only positive connotations. How would you feel if a stranger invaded your domain and suddenly you were locked out of your bedroom? Furthermore, if you take away the customary sleeping space, you must provide the pet with an acceptable alternative and the pet needs time to become accustomed to the new sleeping quarters.

A VISIT TO THE DOCTOR

Your obstetrician isn't the only doctor you need to see during your pregnancy. You need to pay your pet's doctor one last visit before the baby arrives. There are tasks you can take care of now that will save time and effort later.

Before the baby is born, stock up on medications, pet food, shampoo, kitty litter, and any other pet-care necessities. These items have a long shelf life, so they can be stored safely without spoiling. Pet food can be vacuum packed or frozen to extend the freshness date.

Monthly parasite control is important, so be sure to have plenty of this on hand. Have one last fecal examination performed to minimize exposure to intestinal parasites. Deworm your dog or cat if in doubt. Also ask your doctor about monthly heartworm preventatives and monthly flea and tick control products.

Ask the veterinarian to check your pet's teeth. A dental cleaning will reduce the bacterial exposure resulting from the imminent sharing of toys, bottles, and pacifiers.

If your dog or cat will be due for immunizations near the baby's birth date, have these vaccinations administered a little early. Early immunization will not harm the pet and will allow you to check one more thing off of your "to-do list."

BRINGING THE BABY HOME

The big day finally arrives. Bringing the baby home should be a happy event, especially since you are so well prepared for the new family member. But even the best-prepared parents find the first few days after the baby's homecoming are quite hectic.

Homecoming Options

Homecomings are busy times. Friends and relatives file in and out; sleep schedules are disrupted; the household is chaotic. For this reason, some couples choose to board the dog or cat for a few days until the household settles down. This option gives you one less thing to think about. The pet can then be introduced to the changes in the house in a quieter environment.

If you choose not to board the pet, your homecoming needs to be carefully orchestrated. Even though dogs love both their owners, they may be more bonded to one parent than the other. If Fido is more bonded to Mom, then Dad should carry Junior into the house for the first time. That way, Mom can greet Fido and reassure him that his place in the family is secure. The baby is not the center of attention at this initial homecoming event. If Dad is Fido's best friend, simply reverse the roles.

You might also consider having a nonfamily member walk the dog for a few days. You can hire a professional dog attendant, but you may want to ask a neighborhood friend who already knows your dog to help out. Friends are eager to assist new parents, and dog-walking is a good task to delegate. That way your dog still receives ample attention and exercise, you adjust to the new household demands of parenthood, and your friend has the satisfaction of knowing that she is being genuinely helpful.

OK, you have done all your parental homework. The pet has been introduced to the baby bed, the baby toys, the baby lotion, the baby diapers, the baby car seat. Now for the baby!

"Fido, This Is Baby; Baby, This Is Fido"

The first introduction of the baby to the pet should occur in a quiet, controlled environment. Aligning the stars correctly to find this quiet time may take a while, so be patient.

When the right time arises, allow the dog or cat to sniff baby articles first, such as used blankets, diapers, and clothing. They may have had a whiff of "borrowed" baby items, but they need to recognize their "own" baby's smells. If you sent home a baby item from the hospital, you're already ahead of the game.

When introducing these priceless articles, reassure the dog or cat that these smells are acceptable in his world by talking pleasantly to him and petting him. Your earlier efforts to desensitize the pet to new smells will facilitate this process. Remember, these articles are offered only for a sniff and are not to be taken by the pet. If you find your animal grabbing a blanket or other item, a gentle reprimand is in order.

When the actual baby and pet are in the same room for the first time, have the dog controlled on a leash. Have the cat in your arms and on a leash as well to facilitate quick retreat if necessary.

Allow the pet to sniff the baby's feet and monitor his response. If the dog becomes too hyperactive or the cat becomes too agitated, reprimand gently, but firmly, and try again. This may take a while. Introductions cannot be rushed. Quiet acceptance of the baby by the pet should be followed with a reward of praise or treats.

Next, allow the pet the latitude to fully explore the new baby with safeguards still in place. Watch closely as your dog or cat investigates the baby more thoroughly. Be extremely cautious as the pet approaches the baby's face. Face-to-face introductions are sometimes better left for a later date.

Consider the baby's reaction to this introduction as well. If the baby becomes upset or cries, shorten the first session. An upset baby often results in an upset cat or dog. Wait until the baby is calm to continue the introduction. A delayed good introduction is better than a timely bad one.

Gradually expose the pet to the baby in different areas of the house so that he becomes accustomed to the various events surrounding a day in the life of an infant: feeding time, bathing time, changing time, nap time.

The Unbreakable Rule

Even when you are quite comfortable with your pet's response to your new baby, you should remember one essential rule: NEVER LEAVE THE BABY ALONE WITH THE PET. Unpredictable events can provoke unpredictable responses from pets and from babies. Do not take unnecessary risks.

Children need constant supervision when in the presence of a pet. If your pet and baby are in the same room and you need to leave that room, always take one of them with you—the pet or the baby. Even the most trusted pets have caused harm to defenseless infants. In this case, it is better to err on the side of caution.

When dealing with older, more-mobile babies, parents should keep in mind that small children do not understand how their actions will be interpreted by the pet. A child isn't experienced enough to recognize the dog's body language and cannot anticipate that innocent actions may provoke a harmful reaction from the pet. How is a twelve-month-old leaning on the dog in an attempt to pull herself up supposed to know that pressing down on the dog's withers is interpreted as aggression? How is the baby who snatches his teething ring from the dog's mouth supposed to know that he may provoke a defensive canine response? Even when you have done all you can to teach your pet that aggression is not acceptable, close supervision of baby and pet should be exercised.

DANGEROUS PETS

Almost all pets can, using the measures outlined in this chapter, be prepared to safely accept the presence of a new baby in the household. Sadly, though, some cannot. There will also be some for whom parents have not, for whatever reason, provided adequate preparation.

It is always the responsibility of parents to accurately assess the danger a pet might pose and to take steps to protect the baby before an injury occurs. If you see your dog stand dominantly over the baby, be alert to the potential for danger. If you notice your dog twitching his tail, raising his hackles, or barking aggressively, take precautions. A child injured by a "loving" dog is injured nonetheless.

The number of dog bite victims in the United States varies with the study conducted, but all the statistics say the same thing: There are too many dog bite cases and most of them involve children. A CDC (Centers for Disease Control and Prevention) survey estimated that dogs bite nearly 2 percent of the population annually.[2] Dog bites are the second most frequent cause of childhood emergency-room visits. Dog-related injuries lie right behind baseball injuries and ahead of general playground accidents.[3] A dog bite to a child is a physical and emotional trauma.

Even though dog-related injuries are in the spotlight, let's not forget the potential for harm from our feline friends. Cats are not usually associated with fatalities, but they can cause injuries. Cats are often quick to respond to an annoyance with a swipe of the paw and will sometimes bite, too. So the rule of supervised contact pertains to cats as well as dogs. Don't be lulled into a false sense of security and leave your infant and your cat alone in a room. Remember the unbreakable rule— when you leave a room, take either the pet or the baby along with you.

As much as you want to keep the pet in your newly expanded family, be realistic. Injury to a child is a true tragedy, one that cannot always be prevented by pet training. *When in doubt, the pet is out.*

SMOOTH SAILING

Once the household settles into a new routine, it's time to work at including the pet and the baby together in daily activities. What fun is in store for your pet. There are all sorts of entertaining activities such as feeding time and bath time and diaper-changing time. These tasks provide good opportunities to devote attention to the pet and the baby simultaneously.

Make the pet feel part of the entire household routine. Even though it is human nature to pay attention to the pet while the baby takes a nap and you finally have a free minute to spare, avoid this tendency. If you ignore the pet when the baby is present and play with him when the baby is absent, what kind of impression are you giving the pet? The pet will associate the presence of the baby with neglect and the absence of the baby with attention. This is almost certain to have a negative effect on the baby-pet relationship.

By following a few simple steps you can easily include your pet in the care of the infant. For example, your pet will appreciate eye contact while you sit to feed the baby. Simply glance up from the baby occasionally and look at your pet. And since you will speak to your pets and your baby in the same endearing voice, it's easy to verbally communicate with them at the same time.

While bathing the baby, allow the dog or cat to witness this new ritual. There will be new smells (baby soap, powder, and lotion), new sights (naked baby), and new sounds (giggling baby) to experience. What fun this can be for all involved.

Your pet will more readily accept the time you spend with the baby if you share your attention between them. This is also a great lesson for new parents in the art of multitasking, a talent that will serve you well during the years of parenthood.

One Big, Happy Family

Most baby-pet stories do have happy endings. Much effort is needed to keep the expanding family unit balanced and happy, but the end result is worth it.

Early preparation of the pet and the parents and subsequent preparation of the baby are all important. Otherwise, if things don't work out, something's got to give—and it won't be the baby. Every year, pets are displaced from loving homes after the birth of a child because there wasn't sufficient preparation prior to the baby's birth, and chaos ensued.

How wonderful to watch a child grow up in the company of a beloved dog or cat. Raising a child along with a pet benefits the child, the pet, and the family as a whole. So, even though the preparation needed to integrate pets and children into a household is monotonous and time consuming, the joy that comes with the accomplishment is a satisfactory reward.

CHAPTER SUMMARY

Points to Remember

- Having a pet adds another dimension to human relationships when two people share the joy and responsibilities of pet ownership.
- The household routine faces many changes when an infant is brought into a family. Parents eagerly await the arrival of their baby realizing that life will never be the same for them.
- The family pet is also affected by the addition of the infant. Pets see their "pack" or family unit destabilized by the newcomer and may react adversely if not fully prepared for the baby's arrival.
- Early preparation is the key to successful merging of an infant into a pet-owning household. Preparations need to begin as soon as you know the baby will be joining the household.
- Pretraining prevents the pet from negatively associating changes in the household with the presence of the baby.
- Pretraining should focus on basic obedience and desensitization to the changes that will occur when the baby arrives.

Before-Baby Checklist

√ Refresh obedience commands (sit, stay, down).

√ Set household limits if the pet's normal territory will change after the arrival of the baby.

√ Guard against problems related to possessiveness: teach the pet to relinquish toys or food without snarling or biting.

SECOND TRIMESTER

√ Introduce your dog or cat to the sights, sounds, and smells associated with a baby.

  Set up the nursery early.

  Play baby music (mobile) and a recording of baby vocalizations.

  Rub baby powder and lotion on your hands and interact with the pet.

  "Borrow" noxious smelling baby items (e.g., dirty diapers) to
    introduce to your pet.

√ Enforce household boundaries: teach the pet not to enter any area that will be off-limits after the baby arrives.

THIRD TRIMESTER

Take care of veterinary needs:

√ Stock up on pet food and medications.

√ Have your pet's teeth cleaned if needed and have an intestinal parasite test performed.

√ Vaccinate your pet early if immunizations are due close to the baby's birth.

After-Baby Checklist

√ Consider boarding the dog or cat until the household calms down. If you choose not to board the pet, have the most bonded parent greet the dog

Photo by Lynn Buzhardt

while the other parent carries the baby inside for the first time.

√ Consider hiring a dog walker or ask a neighbor to provide adequate exercise.

√ Introduce the baby and pet gradually in a controlled environment. During introductory sessions, always have the dog or cat on a leash to facilitate quick retreats.

√ Expose the pet to new baby smells such as worn baby clothes and dirty diapers. Include the dog or cat in the baby's daily routine by talking to both the pet and the baby during feeding and bath time.

√ Strictly enforce adopted household restrictions by using behavior training techniques.

√ *Never* leave a pet alone with a baby—always take one with you when you leave a room.

Photo by Linell Champagne

CHAPTER 2

IS THIS THE RIGHT TIME?
Assessing Your Family's Readiness to Acquire a Pet

Not all couples already have a pet before children arrive in the home. Sometimes the issue of acquiring a pet doesn't even arise until your child announces that he or she just *has* to have a cat, dog, or some other pet. Perhaps you also long for a dog or cat like the one you had when you were about your child's age. Or you've been reading or talking to friends and it seems that "everyone" believes that kids and pets just go together. Many magazine and Internet articles tout the developmental benefits of pets for children. You don't want your child to miss out, do you?

Children are always faced with peer pressure, and it is certainly true that children without pets may find themselves different in that respect from many of their peers. A survey completed in 2006 by the American Veterinary Medical Association found that nearly 60 percent of all households in the United States own pets. Similar high rates of pet ownership exist in Australia and western Europe. Even in families without pets, parents voice the belief that companion animals are good for children.[1]

If you are struggling with some practical reasons for not getting a pet right now, you may wonder just how important it is to provide a pet for your child. Or perhaps you question whether this is the best time in your child's development to introduce an animal into the household. If so, this section is for you. Here we provide a brief look at what research has to tell us concerning the benefits that children may derive from growing up with pets.

WHAT WE KNOW AND WHAT WE DON'T

There are many assumptions about the role of pets in children's lives. You've probably heard some of them: Pets teach children to handle responsibility, help them learn compassion, and so on. And, in truth, there is some evidence indicating that companion animals can positively influence children's development.[2] But is it sufficiently strong to suggest that you will be doing your child a disservice if you don't get him or her a pet now? Probably not.

The theoretical perspectives that frame the formal study of child development call for studying children in their natural environment. Clearly, considering the prevalence of pets in households, that environment includes animals. Nonetheless, researchers have largely focused on the human relationships in children's lives, with only a few seeking to better understand the importance of the human-animal bond in children's development. Thus our empirical understanding of the way in which having an animal—or not having one in a culture that clearly values them—may influence children's development is more limited than many people might suppose.[3] It could well be that pets do influence child development in very significant ways and that, as one student of child-pet relationships suggests, science just has not caught up with what appears clear from our collective observations.[4]

Social Development

Support for some assumptions about the benefits of pets for children may be inferred from research findings in other areas of child development. It is well documented, for example, that children develop socially and cognitively through their interaction with others. Companion animals can facilitate social contacts for children. Thus they may indirectly play a role in the development of language and social competence. Pets themselves, in serving as children's play partners, provide another object for interaction and challenge children to use different skills as they seek to communicate nonverbally with Fluffy.[5]

Physical and Mental Development

Boris Levinson, a pioneer in the study of children and animals, has suggested that seeking to follow and play with household pets can stimulate babies' muscle development and crawling.[6] Studies of infants' and toddlers' interactions with companion animals have shown that even very young children are able to distinguish between live and lifelike battery-operated toy animals and that they show more interest in the live animals.[7] The ability of animals to attract and interest children indicates that they can be used to motivate learning and teach children about other living things.[8]

Development of Empathy and Compassion

One of the most common assumptions about the beneficial role of pets in children's development is that they help youngsters develop empathy and compassion. In the limited body of research about children and their pets, several studies have produced scientific evidence in support of this assumption. It does, in fact, appear that people who display greater empathy toward animals are also more empathic toward people. Furthermore, this tendency seems to be linked with a history of childhood experiences with pets.[9] These findings are not, however, sufficiently strong or conclusive as to suggest that children who grow up without pets will necessarily be lacking in empathy. Nonetheless, a European study involving 540 four-, six-, and eight-year-olds found support for a link between pet ownership and children's displaying higher levels of helpful or beneficial behavior toward others. On standardized information questionnaires, mothers of children who owned dogs or cats scored their children significantly higher on measures of prosocial behavior than did mothers of nonpet-owning children.[10]

Empathy is a two-way street. Not only do children with pets learn to be more empathic, they benefit from the empathy they perceive in their pets. Other studies indicate that companion animals serve as important sources of comfort for children in stressful situations. Children, especially girls, who own a cat or dog, have been found to display more coping behaviors including expressing emotions, seeking social support, and solving problems.[11] One study of seven- and ten-year-old children found that they were as likely to confide in their pets as in a sibling.[12]

Psychosocial Development

Some research links pet ownership with the development of positive psychological characteristics in children. In one study of third- through sixth-grade children, for example, those with pets scored higher on measures of autonomy, self-concept, and self-esteem with the highest scores among fifth and sixth graders. The better performance of the older children in the sample led the researchers to conclude that the greatest benefits from pets may be derived as children enter preadolescence.[13]

Another study also suggests that children in middle childhood may benefit the most from their association with companion animals. Preschool children scored lower on scales measuring activity with and interest in animals than did middle school and high school students, and children in elementary school had higher scores in taking responsibility for pet care than did either the preschool or high school youngsters in the sample.[14]

Equality of the Sexes

Pets provide what is perhaps the only gender-neutral, culturally accepted care-giving experience in Western culture. Studies in child development have shown that very young children have an understanding of stereotypically male and female adult roles in our society. Even as preschoolers, boys learn to avoid interaction with dolls and babies and can verbalize that caring for a baby is a "mommy" activity.[15] This may not be true of children's relationships with pets, however.

Some research involving both girls and boys has shown that children consider pet care a suitable activity for both genders. Surveys of parents have also revealed that boys and girls spend about equal amounts of time caring for pets. It is notable that studies conducted in cultures in which sibling care-giving is common have found that children who care for their younger brothers and sisters show greater levels of empathy. In the Western world, caring for pets may provide a way for boys to derive some of the developmental benefits of the care-giving role in a way that is consistent with cultural norms.[16]

Hmm . . . Now What?

Okay, so maybe the research doesn't say you have to run out and get an animal for your child today, but it certainly seems to suggest that pet-owning children have certain advantages. If kids with pets have an edge in developing self-concept, empathy, and social skills, do you want to risk your child's growing up without one? And what about the fact that there seems to be a cultural consensus regarding the benefits of family pet ownership? Given all the facts, shouldn't you just go ahead and get an animal? Isn't this like a lot of other things in life; if you spend too much time thinking about it, you never do it? Maybe so. But if you still have some reservations, keep reading. Take a few more minutes to consider the whole picture.

Yes, some evidence suggests that pets are good for kids. But it is important to note that evidence also indicates that it is possible to be an adequate, even a *good*, parent even if your child does not have a pet. And the science in support of raising kids with pets doesn't tell the whole story. Pet ownership can have a downside for children, too; one that might offset the potential benefits, particularly if your family is not ready to adopt a companion animal.[17]

IS THERE A DOWNSIDE TO PET OWNERSHIP FOR CHILDREN?

Little has been made of the negative consequences of pet ownership from the child's perspective. Adults know that children are upset if a pet is lost, dies, or must be given up, but it is often considered a fleeting trauma, one that is just "a part of growing up." Is this really the case?

Studies that examine pet ownership from the child's perspective, tell us that having to relinquish a cherished pet is "a developmental event of major proportions" for children who are school age and beyond.[18] Children demonstrate significant emotional investment in their pets, often including them as central figures when asked to draw a picture of their family.[19] In one study, a group of seven- and ten-year-old children included an average of two pets each when asked to name the ten most important individuals in their lives.[20]

Children themselves acknowledge worrying about the safety and potential loss of their animals as chief among the negative aspects of owning a pet. The strength of children's attachment to their pets suggests pet ownership exposes them to the possibility of significant trauma should the animal be lost, have to be relinquished, or die. Losing a pet is not just an experience that prepares children for "real" losses later on; it is "a unique form of grief" and should be acknowledged and respected as such.[21]

Weighing the Pros and Cons

OK. Most kids have pets. Most parents think they need pets; pets seem to exert a positive influence on children, but they can also expose children to significant worry and emotional trauma. Now you're really confused, right?

Two undisputable facts provide what are probably the best arguments for getting an animal for your family. First, pet ownership in Western culture is the norm: In general, about 90 percent of children will have a pet at some point during their childhood.[22] At least among American children, the desire for a pet is almost universal.[23] Second, pets are, for the most part, just plain *fun*. They add another dimension to our lives and connect us with the natural world from which, in our increasingly urban society, we have become otherwise disconnected. When you put the positives and negatives on the balance scale, the positive aspects of pet ownership win out—*if* your family is ready to accept the responsibilities of animal ownership.

YOU CAN'T PROTECT YOUR CHILD FROM EVERYTHING

Even with the best planning and most favorable circumstances, no parent can ever ensure that a pet will not die prematurely or otherwise be lost to a child. Pets who were already in the family when a child was born will almost certainly die before the child reaches adulthood. While grieving this loss, children can be helped to understand and accept it as part of the natural cycle of life.

YOU CAN PREPARE THE FAMILY FOR A PET

Parents can greatly diminish the chances of other more catastrophic losses, particularly the likelihood of relinquishment, through a realistic evaluation of their family's readiness for pet ownership before acquiring an animal. Wise parents will look beyond the happy anticipation of a child's joy and excitement at greeting a new puppy or kitten and consider whether the circumstances in their household will promote the long-term enjoyment of a family pet.

Animal relinquishment, abandonment, and euthanasia are, unfortunately, prevalent in the United States. Studies that capture the experiences of people relinquishing animals to shelters have much to tell us about the important considerations in the decision to acquire a companion animal.

Remember, too, that a decision not to get a pet *now* doesn't mean that your family can't get one later. Especially if your children are very young, waiting a bit might be the best alternative. While an estimated 40 percent of children begin their lives in homes with pets,[24] several studies suggest that pets may be most beneficial for children who are at least in elementary school. Even if your child is a bit older, you need to consider some of the most important issues in deciding whether to acquire a pet.

WHO'S IN CHARGE HERE, ANYWAY?

Before you decide to adopt a pet—or not to do so—take some time to ask yourself some important questions. Honestly assess your own level of interest in having an animal. Does the thought fill you with anticipation—or dread? Does everyone in the household want a pet? If you want an animal, but your partner is opposed or indifferent to the idea, what will this mean for the pet and the children later on?

Parents' attitudes toward family pet ownership are predicted in part by their own childhood experiences with animals.[25] Did you have a pet when you were young? Did you enjoy the experience? Do you want another pet? Studies of the relinquishment of companion animals have shown that those that are obtained primarily "for the children" are more likely to be given up than other animals.[26] While families with children are more likely to have an animal, they report being less attached to the pet than do pet owners in households consisting solely of adults.[27] Less attachment can logically be assumed to predict greater likelihood of relinquishment when having a pet becomes inconvenient or the responsibilities greater than anticipated. Regardless of a child's promises to manage all the tasks associated with the care of their new pet, it is the adults in the family, particularly the mothers, who usually wind up with primary responsibility for most of the animal's care.[28] Will that be acceptable in your family? Remember, too, that it is not only pet care that must be managed. Having a pet in households with young children means that parents must devote time to monitoring child-pet interaction to ensure the safety of both child and animal.

Dogs, in particular, will need training, an activity that, at least initially, will require some consistent daily attention. Is there room in your schedule for these activities? People relinquishing dogs to shelters report lack of time as the fourth most prevalent reason for giving up their pet.[29]

Out of Sight, Out of Mind?

If you are planning for a pet to live primarily out of doors, consider how much time can be spent with that animal. Is the old adage "out of sight, out of mind" likely to become a reality? For dogs, spending most of the time outdoors or in a crate has been linked with a greater likelihood of the animal's being relinquished.[30] Dogs are pack animals that require time with "their people" if they are to be happy and enjoyable companions. One survey found that Americans spend nearly 95 percent of their time indoors.[31] If the dog is outside the majority of the time and you are inside, consider what this means for animal-human interaction.

Even if children enjoy being outdoors, they may not be home during the times when outdoor activity usually occurs. Keep in mind that the lifestyles of many American families involve being away from home for ten or more hours a day during the week, often returning after dark during the shorter days of winter. If this sounds like your family, how will a dog fit into your schedule?

Family Relationships

Is the interaction among the members of your household conducive to adding a pet? It is true that a pet can be an important source of solace to a child experiencing the stress of family upheaval. In high-conflict families, however, the addition of an animal may exacerbate already troubled relationships. A child's attachment to a pet provides an area of vulnerability that an abusive parent or sibling can use as a tool for manipulation or coercion.

Divorce is also a fact of life for many children today. It is a sobering reality that, statistically, children in the United States are likely to spend more years with a family pet than with both of their parents.[32] Custody disputes over pets have become sufficiently commonplace to prompt some law schools to offer courses in animal law.[33] If you and the child's other parent are divorced, or if that appears likely, have you discussed what getting a pet will mean? Will the animal accompany the child as he or she moves between homes? If not, what effect will that have on the child's desire to spend time in the nonpet-owning household? What will happen to the pet while the child is away?

KNOWING—AND LEARNING—WHAT YOU DON'T KNOW

Chances are that almost no one gets a pet planning to give it up. That decision is usually made, often reluctantly, when the pet has unanticipated needs or causes problems. Interviews with people relinquishing animals have shown that a substantial number had misconceptions about their pet's needs or its behavior. Many owners, for example, believed that female dogs and cats should be allowed to have a litter of young before being spayed. Others were unaware of behavioral differences associated with breeds or had erroneous beliefs about the underlying causes of animal behaviors.

Chapter 3 provides more detailed information about pet selection and specific issues associated with different types of pets. It is wise for you and your children to learn as much as you can before you make the decision to get *any* pet, whatever it might be.[34]

Good Places to Learn

Take some time to question your own long-held assumptions about animal behavior and the well-intentioned advice of neighbors or family members. Your local librarian should be able to recommend some good basic books about pets and pet care; many veterinarians' offices also have publications available at no charge.

If you have school-age children, involve them in the learning process. Knowing that you are collecting information in order to choose the right pet for your family will help them understand the seriousness of this decision. What's more, should you conclude that now is not the time to add a pet to your family, being able to point to concrete information will make this decision easier for your children to understand.

What Does Your Future Hold?

Reading what the experts say about child-pet relationships constitutes only part of your homework. You must also take into account personal factors. What is in store for you and your family? Is a job change looming? Is one of you going back to graduate school? Are there plans for another baby? Will aging parents likely need care or even be joining your household? Any of these events can impact the lifestyle and familial relationships that are part and parcel of your decision about whether to add a pet to the family at this time.

Moving and landlord issues are the top two reasons people give up their dogs and are among the top five reasons people relinquish cats.[35] If you are living in rented property, what are the policies concerning pets? If you will be moving and will need to be in a rented house or apartment, even for a short time, what is the likelihood that you will be able to locate a property that allows animals? If an international move or a move to the state of Hawaii is a possibility, be aware that stringent quarantine regulations for household pets may apply. Moving, with its accompanying changes in routine and loss of contact with friends, can be unsettling enough for children—and parents—without having to give up the family pet.

It Costs How Much?!

The cost of pet maintenance is the third and fourth most common reason given by dog and cat owners, respectively, for relinquishing their pets. Animals in which owners have made a greater investment, including those that were purchased, have been spayed or neutered, or have had other veterinary care, are less likely to be relinquished.[36]

The cost of caring for a dog over the average life span of twelve years is estimated to be about $12,100.[37] The cost of the daily maintenance of a pet varies widely depending on the animal's size and type. Any pet will add expenses to the household, but some will add more than others. (Information about selecting a specific pet is given in chapter 3.) The possibility of illnesses or injuries should also be considered as they can add substantially to the cost of a pet and are unanticipated expenses.

Most veterinarians are happy to provide information to prospective pet owners about costs associated with routine procedures such as vaccinations, spaying and neutering, and parasite prevention. Payment options for more expensive procedures may be available. Discussing these issues with your local veterinarian is an important part of the decision-making process.

CHAPTER SUMMARY

Points to Remember

- When your child tells you he's the "only one" without a pet, he may be right—almost. An estimated 90 percent of children in Western culture live with a pet at some time during their childhood.
- Some studies indicate that children who are bonded to a pet may display greater levels of empathy with humans; they may also be more apt to develop helping or altruistic behaviors, positive self-concept, and personal independence.
- Children report that they confide in pets and that pets serve as important sources of comfort.
- For children, interaction with pets is not just "practice" for human relationships; animals themselves have importance. The loss of a beloved pet is a significant event for children who are school age or beyond.
- The high incidence of animal relinquishment and abandonment in the United States indicates that many people are not fully prepared to meet the needs of the pets they acquire.
- Practicalities such as time, cost, and impending changes in family circumstances often influence outcomes for family pets and should be considered before acquiring an animal.
- Educating yourself and your children about the needs of a pet is an important part of the decision-making process and decreases the likelihood of pet relinquishment.

Pet Readiness Checklist

The following questions will help you to think realistically about the consequences of acquiring a pet at this time in your life. Identify and resolve any red flags that are raised *before* you get a pet of any kind.

√ A pet is ultimately the responsibility of the parents, not the child. If you don't feel happy anticipation at the thought of getting a pet, perhaps now is not the time.

√ Do all adults in your household want a pet? If not, are they opposed or merely indifferent? How will they react during the inevitable ups and downs of an animal's adjustment in your family?

√ If you are divorced, how will acquiring a pet affect your child's visits to both households and the relationship with the nonpet-owning parent?

√ Will your schedule accommodate walking, feeding, training, monitoring of child-pet interaction, and so on?

√ If you live in rented property, does your landlord allow pets? Are there limits as to the size and type of pet your landlord will accept?

√ Where will your pet stay, primarily? If the animal will be outdoors, how much time will you and your child have to spend with it each day? Remember, pets live 24/7, not just when you or your child is there.

√ Is there a possibility you will be moving? Can your pet be accommodated in your new home? If you are considering an international move (or one to the state of Hawaii), have you checked on animal quarantine requirements and the costs and regulations associated with transporting animals to the new location?

√ Check with your local veterinary clinic about the cost of routine vaccinations, parasite control, and neutering.

√ Visit your local pet supply, grocery store, or veterinary clinic to check prices for food and cat litter. Will these costs fit into the family budget?

√ Take time to educate yourself and your child. Information is as close as your local library, the Internet, or a veterinary clinic.

√ Are other changes on the horizon? Will you be caring for an elderly or ill family member or having another baby? If so, how will these events influence your ability to keep and care for a pet?

Photo by Erin Gleason

Photo by Linell Champagne

CHAPTER 3

A DECISION YOU CAN LIVE WITH
Selecting the Right Pet for Your Child and Family

So your head is spinning with the thought of getting a pet. Will this be the first pet in your family or are you adding yet another one to an existing menagerie? Have you shared your thoughts of getting a pet with the rest of your family? Have you had these pet-related thoughts for a while? Are these thoughts well grounded or is this idea merely a passing whim? If you just can't get the thought of owning a pet out of your mind, it's probably time to think about which pet to get.

The key here is to remember that even though the initial idea may have originated within the deep recesses of *your* mind, this will be a pet for the whole family and every member of the family should be given consideration before making the choice. The best choice may not be your first choice. That sleek sporting dog that Dad has in mind may not make any more sense for your family than a sleek sports car. And just as with cars, parents may have to think more in terms of pet function than image.

There are questions to answer before you ever look at a newspaper ad, visit a breeder, or scout the Web in search for the perfect pet (as if the perfect pet really exists). Do you want a cat, a dog, a bunny, a hamster, an iguana? The choices are almost limitless. Though we briefly address the idea of other pets later in this chapter, our focus is on domestic cats and dogs. So let's look at some of the things to consider before you go pet shopping.

THE DOLLARS AND CENTS OF PET OWNERSHIP

Nothing in this world is free. All pets mean recurring household expenditures.

Purchasing a pet obviously requires an initial investment. But it doesn't stop there. Even give-away pups and kittens come with a price tag. So before you go pet shopping, look at your family budget and calculate the funds that can be moved to the "pet column" of your monthly balance sheet.

How much are you willing to spend to acquire a pet? The cost of a dog or cat varies tremendously, so set a budget and stick to it. Your breed selection may actually be influenced by market price. Do you really want that French bulldog enough to spend $3,500 or will a $450 Boston terrier suffice?

The prices for purebred dogs and cats depend on quality of the pet (you may find a pet-quality dog from a show litter for a lesser fee), popularity of the breed (the law of supply and demand comes into play here; if Persian cats are the "in" breed, expect to pay more), and the size of the litter (owners may be willing to part with the ninth pup in a litter for a little less). Scout the Web and newspaper ads to get a feel for the going price of the breeds you like.

The Adoption Option

If you decide to adopt a pet from a shelter, good for you. Just don't expect the adoption to be free. Adoption fees are usually reasonable, but they do have to be paid.

These fees vary and the funds often support humane organizations, allowing them to care for more displaced pets. Most adoption agencies and humane societies post their fees on their Web sites. The requirements for adoption should be listed, too. Review these carefully so that you will be informed before you visit the shelter or adoption site.

Since many doctors work in conjunction with humane societies, your veterinarian may have information on adoption centers. In fact, many private practitioners care for homeless pets in their hospitals, so ask your veterinarian if he has any pets in need of a good family. Also, check your veterinarian's bulletin board for adoptable pets. Clients often post notices of available dogs and cats there.

When a Pet Chooses You

Sometimes pets choose us instead of the other way around. What should you do if a dog or cat shows up on your doorstep? How do you deal with the child who thinks the finders-keepers maxim prevails?

Stray pets are often named Lucky because they were fortunate to wander up to a home that could keep them. However, they can quickly become *unlucky* if the home is not ready for a new pet. So lay aside the guilt trip, disregard the pleading eyes, and be objective in your decision to keep a stray dog or cat. The list of animal characteristics discussed later in this chapter should also be considered in the case of a stray.

If you are seriously considering keeping a stray, have your veterinarian do a thorough physical examination and parasite check to give you a clearer picture of your potential adoptee. If the pet needs extensive medical care, the family budget may be strained bringing the pet up to par. For example, a dog with heartworms will add a major expense to the household as he undergoes treatment.

A stray that finds a loving home simply by showing up at the right place at the right time is indeed lucky. You just need to be certain that your house is the right place and now is the right time for you.

The More the Merrier?

If one pet in a household is good, are two even better? Many people consider adopting or purchasing pets in pairs. This works for many families, but beware of the potential difficulties in store.

People that acquire more than one pet at a time do so for a variety of reasons. They may think that the pets will provide company for each other. Families that spend a majority of the day away from the house often feel this way. In addition, some parents with more than one human child look for a "pet per child." They think that each child needs an individual pet. Still others simply enjoy observing the camaraderie and interaction between the pets.

Certainly there can be benefits to owning more than one pet. And many families can maintain more than one pet. Just be aware that multiple pets mean more time and more expense. Also, be alert to the establishment of a pet hierarchy in your household. There can be only one alpha pet. It's difficult to have a happy home if the pets squabble constantly.

The Fertility Fee

Some breeders and adoption agencies require your commitment to spay or neuter the pet. This may be to prevent overpopulation, ensure breed quality, or both. Adoption agencies may include this surgery expense in the adoption fee or may already have spayed or neutered the pet prior to adoption. Find out if a reproduction fee is incorporated into the adoption fee or if it will be an additional expense.

If you purchase a dog or cat that has not been spayed or neutered, the surgical expense may not be incurred until the pet is several months old, and it will be a one-time investment. You need to add it to the cost of the pet, nonetheless. Check with your pet's doctor if you already have one or call local veterinarians for an estimate of reproductive surgery so that you can include it in the calculated cost of a pet.

Tuition Costs

Another one-time (hopefully) expense to consider is obedience training. You want this pet to be in your family for a long time, and ill-mannered dogs and cats usually find themselves looking for another home in short order. Depending on the length and type of obedience sessions, expect to spend one hundred to four hundred dollars on training. Investigate local obedience classes before you begin pet shopping.

Many obedience trainers offer refresher courses at no extra cost, so shop carefully. It's a good idea to visit several obedience schools and watch the teacher in action before making a choice. Note how the trainer interacts with the dogs and how the owners and pets respond to the teaching method. Don't be afraid to ask for references and check them out. A reputable trainer will welcome this scrutiny. Beware of trainers that rely heavily on aversive correction methods rather than on positive reinforcement for good behavior. Obedience school should be a productive, fun experience for both the pet and the pet owner as well as providing socialization opportunities for your dog.

The Cost of Food and Health Care

After the initial expenditures, there will be additional, recurring expenses associated with your pet. For example, there will always be food to buy.

Pet food can be a significant expense, so feeding the dog or cat should probably be figured into the monthly family food budget. After all, the pet is part of the family, right? Commercial pet foods vary in quality and cost, with premium foods commanding a premium price. Even so, your pet's food bill should not be extraordinarily high, considering that she doesn't dine out or ask to breeze through a fast food drive-through.

Immunizations and parasite control will be recurring expenses. Vaccinations are usually more expensive for pups and kittens receiving the initial series of immunizations, but even older dogs and cats need occasional boosters.

As for parasite prevention, young pets need more frequent dewormings, but you should expect to buy monthly parasite medication for the life of the pet. Monthly, comprehensive parasite control medications are important for the health of the pet as well as for the health of your family (see chapter 6).

For an estimate of immunization and parasite control medications, call your veterinarian so you can figure this expense into your pet budget. On average, expect to spend two hundred to four hundred dollars per year on parasite control medications and immunizations.

FAMILY SURVEY: WHAT PET SHOULD YOU CONSIDER?

When you've decided that your thoughts of pet ownership are not fleeting and you've ascertained that your family can afford a pet, the next step is to actually choose one. But how do you decide which kind of pet to get? Start by taking a good look at the current members of your family (human and otherwise) before you look at adding a dog or cat.

How old are the children? If they are old enough to have a reasonable opinion rather than an exaggerated wish ("I really, really do want a pet elephant!"), let them have a say. To motivate serious thought on which pet to get, conduct a family survey. Family surveys keep you focused and allow everyone to express an opinion.

Ask your family members what kind of dog or cat they might like in general. For older children, opinions may be based on pets they've encountered at the homes of friends. For younger children, opinions may be entirely based on the latest movie they've seen. And the average household pet, like the average pet owner, never turns out to be just like the movie. So parents should provide a reality check.

Weigh the preferences and opinions of your children and discuss the following points in your survey:

What size pet do you want?
How old should the pet be? (Puppy, kitten, adult pet?)
What breed do you want? What "look" do you like?

What are your family's interests or hobbies and where will the pet fit
   in with those?
How much time will the family have to spend with the pet?
How big is your house? Will the pet live inside?
How big is your yard? Is your yard fenced or can it be fenced? If you
   don't have a yard, where will you walk your pet?

Engaging your children in a discussion of these practical aspects of pet ownership can forestall impulsive choices and give them a better understanding of
the pet's needs. If your children are old enough, encourage them to read about
prospective pets in the library or on the Internet and report back to the family
about what they learn. Then you can all discuss how the characteristics of that
particular pet might match with your family's preferences and circumstances.

Size Does Matter

Let's think about size and how it relates to a new cat or dog in your household.
When looking for a cat, the size range is relatively consistent. Within a few
pounds, cats are approximately the same size, but when considering dogs, the
size range is huge. And bigger is not always better when it comes to dogs.
What size dog can your house and yard accommodate? What size dog will your
children feel comfortable with in their home? Just because your four-year-old
wants the Saint Bernard that starred in her favorite movie doesn't mean this
large dog will work in your family.

BIG DOGS

Don't fall for the "precious puppy persuasion." If you have a thirty-five-pound
toddler, understand that the cute little fifteen-pound golden retriever puppy
he fell in love with will quickly outgrow him. Will your child be overwhelmed
by the seventy-five-pound dog that gallops across the yard like a small pony?

Size differential is an important factor when there are very young children
in the house. Even the gentlest of large dogs can be intimidating to a small
child. And scared children rarely enjoy their dogs. Families have to work with
the beginning and ending size of the pets they choose. Children are often the
smallest breathing creature in the house. Do you think they may like being the
"bigger" one for a change? How about considering a smaller canine variety?

Sometimes, very young children fair better with midsize dogs. Medium-size dogs are often the "happy medium." The dog is not big enough to cause "casual harm," the type of harm that can occur when the full-grown Rhodesian ridgeback on his way to the food bowl accidentally bumps into a small child. And a midsize dog is not as apt to be injured by a rambunctious toddler either.

LITTLE DOGS

We usually focus on the harm a dog may cause, but injury is a two-way street. Size matters here, too. Many parents avoid getting very small dogs for fear that the child may harm the dog. A very tiny dog may sustain unintentional injury at the hands of the child. Imagine a two-pound toy poodle pup being accidentally dropped down the stairs by a pair of three-year-old hands or being run over by a tricycle going full blast.

That's not to say that very large and very small dogs are never good pets for children—they can be. But parents have to be aware of and make accommodations for the size differential. The dog and the child both need education and protection to make the big versus little situation work.

SIZING UP CATS

Size is not a significant factor when choosing a cat. Most adult cats weigh between five and fifteen pounds. But this means cats start out and remain the smallest member of the family. Even a toddler looms large over a cat.

Luckily, cats are very good at avoiding injury at the hands of a child by simply avoiding the child altogether. Cats can jump vertically or crawl into nooks and crannies that are inaccessible to children (at least most children). Felines usually find a safe haven somewhere in the house where they can be undisturbed. So if cats top your pet shopping list, you can delete the size issue from your family survey. But there are other considerations in choosing a cat.

Young Pets or Old?

What about the age of the pet? Nothing says that all families should start with a puppy or kitten. Many families do quite well with adult dogs or cats.

If you do want a younger pet, look for one at least eight weeks old. Pups and kittens should nurse for approximately six weeks to derive the benefits of natural protection from the antibodies in their mother's milk. That allows two weeks for weaning before they are separated from their loving food source. Waiting until the pet is a couple of months old also provides time for in-litter socialization, which may have an effect on the pet's personality.

Some people prefer to let the dog or cat get quite a bit older before taking him into their family. Lots of pet lovers would rather start with an older pet, one that is already housebroken and perhaps a little calmer.

Acquiring an adult pet can be a win-win situation. You give a home to an adult pet that may otherwise have difficulty being adopted. You reap the rewards of having someone else go through all the housebreaking and litter box–training hassle. And you may just find the ideal pet for your family.

If you choose an adult pet, it comes with a past, so get a full medical history. You need to know about its previous vaccinations and health issues. For cats and dogs, inquire about the status of intestinal parasite and heartworm tests. Ask if the pet has been consistently given monthly heartworm prevention. For cats, also inquire about feline immunodeficiency virus and feline leukemia virus test results. Adopting an older pet is like buying a used car: It may be the best choice, but it can come with preexisting problems.

While thinking about age, consider the overall life expectancy of the pet. Pets have shorter life spans than do humans, and your child will have to eventually deal with pet loss. If you choose an eight-year-old dog or a twelve-year-old cat, your child may have to deal with death even sooner. A young adult pet, between one and three years of age, is probably a better choice if your child is very young.

Age at adoption is one consideration for life expectancy, but it's not the only one. Different breeds have different life expectancies. While you cannot predetermine when any pet will meet his end, you can review information regarding average life expectancy by breed and choose a pet that fits into your general family plan. Researching a specific breed will provide life expectancy data, but in general, remember that the larger the dog, the shorter the life. A Great Dane will usually not survive as long as a miniature poodle.

Although the life expectancies of cats may vary with breed, they are more consistent than dogs. Many cats have very long lives (even without counting all nine of them), and it is not unusual to have a healthy cat remain a family member for eighteen to twenty years.

The issue of longevity sometimes may need to be addressed from another angle. Since lots of couples have a pet before they have children, the pet may be up in years when the child is born. Parents are concerned that their children will have difficulty dealing with the imminent death of a senior pet. You will find information on dealing with pet loss in chapter 7.

Beauty or the Beast? How Will Your Pet Look?

Pets come in so many varieties that the choices can be staggering. And if beauty is in the eye of the beholder, which pet do you want to behold? Let's review some appearance options.

HAIRDOS: WHAT TYPE HAIR WILL DO?

Does your family want a long-haired pet or a short-haired pet? Do you prefer short-coated terriers, long-haired collies, or gussied-up poodles? How much pet hair in the house can you tolerate?

Contrary to what you may have heard, there is no breed of dog that doesn't shed at all. (Even a Mexican hairless has a little hair.) Hair shafts go through a cycle that includes release from the hair follicle, so all hair eventually falls out. Some breeds, like poodles may not shed as much as others, but they *all* shed. Healthy coats, however, do shed less. Forget the magic potions and consult your veterinarian about keeping your pet's coat, regardless of its length, healthy.

As with people, longer hair may require more maintenance. Long-haired cats and dogs need to be brushed regularly to prevent matted fur and to remove "dead" hair before it falls out all over the sofa. Hair dressing takes time. If you don't have time to put your toddler's hair in a fresh pony tail during the morning frenzy, how will you find time to brush a Persian cat or a Shetland sheepdog? Add a little extra to the time commitment section of the family survey if you want a long-haired pet.

Add a little to the expense section of the survey, too. Grooming services are sometimes required for long-haired pets. This means another recurring pet-related expense that should be factored into the family budget.

Grooming prices vary, but cat owners should consider a trip to the groomer to bathe, comb out, and clip a cat to start at about forty dollars. Some cats don't like the sound of electric clippers and require light anesthesia, which increases this cost further.

Grooming dogs will depend on the size of the dog and the condition of the coat. Keeping your dog combed will save you money since groomers charge for the extra time it takes them to comb out tangles. Pet owners can expect to spend a minimum of thirty dollars to bathe, clip, and comb out their dogs, but it's not unusual for grooming fees to be seventy-five to one hundred dollars—and even higher for larger dogs. Grooming a miniature poodle does not cost the same as grooming a standard poodle.

A NOSE FOR THE RIGHT DOG

There are other physical characteristics to ponder besides coat. Believe it or not, the length of the dog's nose and the position of the eyes are important considerations.

A short-nosed, bulging-eyed dog (e.g., Pekingese) or cat (e.g., Persian) will be susceptible to ocular injury. These forward-positioned eyes are like the headlights of a car—they catch everything that goes by, including circulating dust, little fingers, and flying toys. Corneal abrasions and ulcerations are common in these brachycephalic (short-nosed) breeds. These eye injuries require medical treatment, which is often costly, and they may result in vision impairment. So expect eye problems and be prepared to handle them as they occur.

When it comes to brachycephalic breeds, you often hear them before you actually see them. Short-nosed breeds like bulldogs and Boston terriers make a respiratory noise that can be disconcerting. Some people find it difficult to sleep next to a snorting, snoring dog. And remember—even if the dog sleeps with your child in another room, you'll still be able to hear his nocturnal utterances over the baby monitor.

These respiratory noises are often related to allergies and may be decreased with medication, but others are due to the strange anatomy of the brachycephalic's larynx. Some particularly serious cases require surgery on the larynx or respiratory tract. But even with medical or surgical intervention, you can expect a little snoring. Of course, many people think this adds to the dog's character. Even so, you need to consider eyes and noses in pet selection.

Will You and Your Dog Have Anything in Common?

What are your family's interests? What do you like to do individually and as a family group? Will the pet fit in with your family? Your family survey should include a look at your family's collective personality and interests.

Photo by Linell Champagne

If your family is the outdoors type and likes to camp and hike, a working or herding breed may be a good fit. These dogs enjoy outdoor activity. If you spend your life on the noisy sidelines of a soccer field or in the stands of a baseball park, perhaps a sedate mixed breed would be better. Some dog breeds simply ignore the frenzy. If your family is studious and prefers to sit on the sofa and read, perhaps you should consider a cat.

Are you a family of runners or walkers? Do you want an athletic dog that can jog five miles with you? Think about a Labrador, greyhound, or whippet. Or do you live in small quarters and want a short-legged dog that may have trouble keeping up on a brisk family walk but will be a good inside playmate? Perhaps a dachshund is in your future.

IS YOUR FAMILY "FIT" FOR A PET?

Exercise is always the first component in a fitness plan, whether for humans or animals. In surveying your family, assess, the time you have available to exercise—yourself *and* the dog. While you're at it, assess your physical ability to exercise with your dog. Can you keep up with a long-legged greyhound or should you opt for a breed with a little less zip?

Dogs living outside can exercise without their owners if they are so in-

Photo by Anne Guedry

clined, but even outside dogs in large yards need us to motivate them. Even the most energetic, bird-chasing dog will rarely exercise enough on his own. Bird chasing may get boring and the shady spot under the elm tree may be a little too enticing. Inside dogs have very little opportunity for exercise on their own unless they run laps around the dining room table. They definitely need owners to organize physical activity.

The degree of exercise required varies by breed, so think about the time your family has to devote to a canine exercise program before choosing a dog. Lots of adults can't find time to go to the gym themselves much less work out with the dog.

ENERGY ASSESSMENT: THE DOG'S, NOT YOURS

Positive energy is a good thing, but some dogs positively have too much energy. It's a good idea to find a dog with an energy level that matches your own.

If a rambunctious border collie chasing bicycle wheels is not what you're after, stay away from herding dogs. If you prefer not to have the doorbell's ring compounded by a series of sharp yelps, perhaps you should look past the toy fox terrier. If you cannot deal with a goofy Labrador until he "matures," find another dog.

There are calm dogs—you simply have to look for them. Some dogs may be calmer by nature, but most dogs can be trained to curb bursts of energy. So don't mistake lack of discipline for hyperactivity. Most dogs can be trained to behave if you are willing to take the time to do so *and* provide sufficient exercise.

Nurture versus Nature: Are Some Dogs Inherently Mean?

No one wants to purchase or adopt a "mean" companion animal. But what makes a dog "mean"? Is he born mean or does the manner in which he is raised determine his temperament? Are certain breeds inherently more dangerous than others?

While any breed of dog can be dangerous, certain breeds may have unique behavioral tendencies. Carefully research breed temperaments before pet shopping. But remember, any breed of dog that is not socialized or trained properly may pose a risk.

Dogs may not be born mean, but pups that are kept confined and denied sufficient socialization often have temperament issues. Pups need to be nurtured by their canine mother and socialized with their siblings. They also need human contact from an early age.

EARLY SOCIALIZATION

Puppies should not be removed from their mothers until they are at least seven to eight weeks of age. One of many things that pups learn during the time with their mom and littermates is bite inhibition. Bites that hurt are answered with nips from the mother or a sibling so that puppies learn how hard is too hard. Sufficient time in the litter may also be a factor in a pup's learning to interact more positively with other dogs. So be wary of a breeder who is willing to let you have a just-weaned pup.

If you acquire a dog or cat from a breeder, take a good look around. Is the young animal confined to a cage all day or does the owner spend time with him and raise him like "family"? Does he have play time with his siblings? If he is the only one in the litter, has he been exposed to other dogs or cats? Look for pups and kittens raised in a family atmosphere that have been exposed to lots of human and animal contact from birth.

If you shop for a pup or kitten in a pet store, ask about his family history. Did he come from an individual breeder or was he born in a puppy mill or large cattery and taken away from his mother too soon? These same questions should be addressed if you adopt a pup or kitten from a shelter.

Ask about how the shelter came to have the animal and what shelter staff have observed about its behavior during the time it has been there. Animal rescue organizations often have staff that are skilled in evaluating animals' behavior and temperament. Spend some time with them talking about your family's lifestyle and expectations of a pet so they can help you select an animal that's right for you. Most reputable rescue organizations will insist on this anyway before they send you out the door with a pet.

If you are planning to select a puppy, take some time to read or talk with your veterinarian about evaluating a puppy's temperament. The puppy that immediately leaves his littermates to run and greet you may appear to have picked you to be his family; in fact, however, such behavior could indicate a dominant pup who may be more disposed to difficult or willful behavior.[1] Find out more about him and his littermates before you make a final decision.

BEWARE OF DOG!

Breed alone does not determine temperament. Nurture (training, socialization) and nature (genetics) both play an important part. However, some dogs are more likely to inflict harm than others. Let's look at a few facts related to dog-inflicted injuries.

Dog bites are the second most frequent cause of childhood emergency room visits, second only to playground accidents such as baseball and softball injuries.[2] Approximately 77 percent of dog bites incurred by children are in the area of the head and neck.[3] And don't think that "strange" dogs are at fault; 80 to 90 percent of bites were inflicted by dogs known to the children.[4]

Injury rates are higher for children between the ages of five and nine. The likelihood of being bitten by a dog decreases as the age of the child increases. Boys are more likely to be the victim of a dog bite than are girls. This tendency may be related to the manner in which young boys play.[5] But girls are bitten by dogs, too. Children of both sexes are more likely to be bitten by a dog than are adults because of several factors.

First, children usually play with dogs more than adults do, and children have more free time at home. They aren't preparing dinner or balancing the checkbook. Second, children sometimes unintentionally provoke the dog by their darting movements and loud voices during play. Third, children are less experienced when it comes to interpreting a dog's signs of aggression. They might not realize that when tails point up and ears point forward, trouble may lie ahead. Finally, small children are less able to defend themselves against aggressive attacks by dogs than are larger adults.

So which dogs are more aggressive? Statistically, certain breeds are associated with more human injuries than others. This is not breed prejudice—it's just fact. Pit bulls are credited with the most serious or fatal human bites of all breeds. Rottweillers come in second. Other breeds noted for aggressiveness are chows, Akitas, huskies, and bullmastiffs.[6] But to be fair, a large number of nonfatal dog bites are inflicted by good old mixed-breed dogs. No dog is beyond biting under certain circumstances.[7]

As long as there are dogs, there will be dog bites. Your job as a parent is to recognize this fact: All dogs can bite. Review the statistics, choose your dog wisely, and train him well. Teach your children how to behave around dogs, too. Then the fear of a dog bite doesn't have to overshadow the joy of having the dog.

Cat-related injuries are usually not discussed as much as dog-induced injuries because they are seldom fatal, but cats can and do inflict harm. Cats should be socialized, like dogs, with their littermates as well as humans to provide a solid foundation for good behavior.

WHERE WILL THE PET ACTUALLY RESIDE?

Several questions on your family survey should pertain to a single topic— where will your cat or dog live? Will he be an outside pet or inside pet? Will the dog or cat have dual residency with free access to both the home and the yard? Can you envision your back door with a "doggy door" insert? Are the house and yard large enough to accommodate your pet of choice?

Outside Accommodations

Ahh . . . the great outdoors. What you see as every dog's dream could turn into your biggest nightmare. Think about the size of your yard and the proximity to neighbors while deciding which pet to get and where it will live. Believe it or not, the great outdoors isn't so great for lots of pets. Since lots of cats live indoors, let's focus on outside dogs for the time being.

Although dogs aren't terribly impressed by a well-manicured lawn and expensive shrubbery, a barren landscape of a yard isn't what most dogs want to call home. Outdoor space must be adequately prepared to accommodate a dog safely and securely. And look beyond the scope of your own yard. What about your neighbors? Will they be dog-friendly, or will they complain every time the dog barks at a bird?

While you don't need to clear the back forty for the new dog, when it comes to yards, size *does* matter to your pet, to you, and to your neighbor. First, for the pet, it's not fair to contain an energetic, seventy-pound golden retriever in a postage stamp–size yard. Large dogs, especially more athletic breeds, need room to run. Even if you plan to provide the dog with an intense, organized exercise regimen, he still needs a little room to stretch between workouts. So take a good look at your backyard before pet shopping. Is there enough room for a large breed dog or should you put a smaller breed at the top of your shopping list?

How about your own considerations; can you stand the cleanup detail necessary to keep a large dog in a small yard? And what about your neighbor? If your neighbor's house sits two feet from your own, he may appreciate your acquiring a smaller pet—and a quiet one.

Regardless of yard size, outside dogs need protective shelter, so shop around a little to determine the cost of housing. There are many varieties of ready-made dog houses available or you may take the construction of a dog house on as a family project. At any rate, houses cost money, so add this expense to the projected pet budget.

Please Fence Me In

Fencing the backyard is yet another factor to think about prior to your dog search. Although dogs may love to run in wide open spaces, fences provide security for them. And to fence or not to fence may not even be an option. Fencing is a requirement in many locales that have ordinances prohibiting free-roaming dogs.

Fences provide security by keeping your dog in and, depending on the fence, keeping other dogs out. Dogs that can't reach each other can't fight. And fences keep your dog off the street. Domestic dogs that aren't streetwise quickly become victims of the dreaded HBC (veterinary terminology for "hit by car"). In addition to security, a fenced-in yard provides the pet with an anytime exercise area and an array of interesting diversions to stave off boredom.

Before you select a dog, select a fence. Decide on the type of fence and get a couple of cost estimates so you can keep within your pet budget. For some yards, traditional fences may be the best and less expensive choice, while for others an underground electronic fence may win the family vote. Consider that underground electronic fences do not protect your pet from animal or human intruders and that some dogs learn that running through them can yield hours of freedom in exchange for only a moment of pain. On the plus side, electronic fences eliminate the risks posed by gates left ajar or dogs who learn to excavate escape tunnels.

Once installed, the cost of upkeep for either fence type is minimal, so there are no significant recurring expenses. Nonetheless, keep in mind that traditional fences do need occasional painting or weatherproofing and replacement batteries for electronic collars may run thirty to sixty dollars every three to four months, so both will slightly increase the cost of pet care.

Inside Accommodations

If you decide that your pet will live inside, you have far less work to do and, with proper planning, virtually no additions to the pet budget; however, there are a few things that you need to consider.

Inside pets need personal space. They need a quiet place to eat and sleep and firm boundaries set so they know where they are allowed to go when they are not eating or sleeping. Provide your cat or dog with an area all his own where he can retreat from household activity at will. A corner of the laundry room or a bathroom may be a good choice for your pet. The private space should provide comfortable bedding, food and water, plus a litter pan for our feline friends.

Think about exactly where your pet will sleep for the night. Will he be allowed to sleep in a family member's bed, on the sofa, on the rug in the den? Pets that roam during the night can disrupt the sleep of the entire family, so teach your pet where he should sleep.

Which areas of the house will be considered his territory during waking hours? Will he be allowed in the formal living room? Will Grandma's handmade quilt in the master bedroom be off-limits? Have everyone in the family agree on boundaries so that the entire family can enforce them consistently.

Pets don't do well with mixed signals, and having to replace the antique Persian rug in the dining room really adds to the pet budget.

Increased family-pet interaction occurs when well-behaved pets are allowed access around the house, but disaster can occur when they are not trained properly or when boundaries are not respected. Harmonious family-pet living environments require give and take—you give the direction and the pet takes you seriously.

BEYOND THE BASICS

How would an alternative pet fit into your household? Pets come in many varieties from hamsters, to guinea pigs, iguanas, birds, ferrets, and rabbits. These pets are small and take up very little space in the house. Even though they don't take up much room, their cages still need to be cleaned, so assess your commitment to pet housekeeping in your family survey.

Alternative pets vary greatly and so do their needs. Explore the species thoroughly, learning what they eat, their life expectancy, and their specific health care issues. Also consider the degree of bonding your child will have with an exotic pet. Your child may love that parakeet, but will the two of them develop a close relationship? Will that hamster snuggle on the sofa with your child? Will that iguana ask to be petted? Some research suggests that children become more attached to dogs and cats, possibly because they are typically more interactive.[8]

Research the incidence of human injuries inflicted by exotic pets. Ferrets are often associated with infant bites. Birds, especially large birds, have tremendous tensile strength in their beaks that can snap little fingers. Frightened rabbits have strong rear legs that can scratch young arms.

Rabbits and other small exotic pets can also be unintentionally harmed by young children who "hug too hard." Rabbits are especially prone to injury at the hands of exuberant children. Children try to hold on tight when hugging soft bunnies. When the bunny grows tired of snuggling it may struggle to get free. As he pushes against the child with those powerful rear legs, the bunny may break his own back. This can be a fatal injury. Children that own rabbits should be mature enough to understand the safe handling of their pets and to accept that most rabbits do not enjoy being held.

An alternative pet may be a good choice when space is an issue. You don't need to worry about the size of your yard and you don't need to live near a park to exercise these small pets. They also fit in well with busy family schedules since they require little maintenance. So you may want to add the possibility of an alternative pet to your family survey and consider more than just cats and dogs. But remember that such pets may have very specific needs. So take the time to learn what those needs are and consider how your family will meet them.

REFINING YOUR OPTIONS

With your family survey completed, your family budget and accommodations assessed, and your home environment evaluated, you have a better idea of the pet you want and the accommodations that you will need to make in order to get him. With your pet options sufficiently narrowed, the next step will be a trip to the veterinary clinic.

Don't feel foolish going into a veterinary clinic without an animal in tow. This is a question-and-answer session, and the veterinarian will be happy to chat with you.

A visit to the veterinarian should begin and end your pet-shopping venture. When you take time to ask specific questions regarding breeds you are considering, your doctor can effectively educate you on choosing the healthiest pet. Your veterinarian will give you a list of physical and behavioral characteristics to look for in your breed of choice and a few to avoid.

In addition to veterinarians, Internet sites are often very informative. You can converse with people who actually have a particular breed that interests you. Just make sure the Web sites are reputable, valid sources of information, in addition to offering anecdotal stories of other pet owners.

And remember the gold standard of information—the public library. You will be amazed at the number of good books available that deal with specific kinds of dogs, cats, and other pets.

Scouting Expedition

After visiting your veterinarian and doing your other research, make a list of kennels or adoption agencies or pet stores you want to visit. Make the first visit without the children, so that you can make an objective appraisal of the pet without succumbing to the "please, can I have him?" litany. Prospective pet owners should screen the pup or kitten for obvious medical problems on site. Ask your veterinarian what to look for in a healthy pet. Once you pick out a pup or kitten, have the veterinarian do a thorough physical examination as soon as possible.

A Discerning Eye

What *should* you look for in a pet? It's relatively simple. Start with a cursory examination. Look at the animal's coat. Is it shiny? Or dull and flaky? Are there any abrasions or sores on the skin? Are there any bald spots visible?

Watch the pet move around. Does he bear equal weight on all four legs or does he limp? All pups and kittens are a little clumsy and hop around, so don't mistake normal juvenile ambulation for orthopedic problems. Gently feel the top of the head. Is there a soft spot? Unlike soft spots in human babies, this defect in the skull may not close as the puppy or kitten grows up.

Look at the eyes—are they clear or bloodshot? Do the eyes have a discharge? Look at the ears—and smell them too; odors from the ears often indicate infection.

Look at the gums—are they pink or pale? Does the puppy or kitten have an underbite or an overbite? Look at the tummy—are there any bulges? Protrusions from the abdominal wall may mean that the youngster has a hernia.

Does the pup or kitten play or seem sullen? Does he have a good appetite? What specific kind of food is he eating? Has he had any diarrhea or vomiting?

Once you have ascertained the health of your new family member to the best of your ability, proceed to your veterinarian for a more thorough examination.

Getting the Veterinarian's Input

Your veterinarian will perform what's known as a prepurchase exam. Note the prefix "pre." You may have already laid out a significant amount of money for the dog or cat, but the transaction should not be sealed until the pet is thoroughly examined. Most reputable breeders, pet stores, and adoption agencies will allow a two- to four-day prepurchase window to provide you ample opportunity to visit the veterinarian and confirm the health status of the dog or cat before finalizing the sale.

It's important to make the earliest veterinary appointment possible. In fact, it's sometimes best to have the new pet see the veterinarian before it ever sets one of its four feet inside your home. That way, if the pet is not medically sound, he can be returned before a long-lasting attachment is developed. But who are we kidding? Most people fall in love on the car ride to the animal hospital.

What will your veterinarian look for? The doctor will look for the same characteristics you did and will examine the dog or cat thoroughly for:

1. Ocular problems including abnormalities of the cornea, iris, lens, retina, and eyelids
2. Teeth and bite formation (underbite or overbite)
3. Hard palate defects such as cleft palates
4. Nasal passage occlusions or discharge
5. Ear infections or ear mite infestations
6. Skin lesions related to mange mites, fleas, and fungal or bacterial infections
7. Inguinal or umbilical hernias
8. Undescended testicles in males
9. Lymph node enlargement that may indicate infection
10. Abdominal abnormalities
11. Heart murmurs
12. Inappropriate lung sounds
13. Orthopedic irregularities, open fontanels (soft spot on skull), or conformation problems
14. Neurologic abnormalities
15. Intestinal parasites

Once your pup or kitten gets a clean bill of health, your veterinarian will give you an owner-orientation talk. He will discuss many topics including nutrition, behavior, and general health care.

The first topic may be the staff of life—food. Not all foods are created equal. When it comes to pet food, you often do get just what you pay for. Your veterinarian will suggest a good food for your particular pet. Follow her advice on what brand to feed and heed the feeding schedule.

WILL YOU SAY "YES" TO A PET?

Growing up with a pet can be a joy—for children and parents alike. But as pet care is ultimately the responsibility of the adults in the home, parents need to objectively evaluate their commitment to pet ownership as a major part of the overall family survey.

Do you have sufficient time to train and care for a pet? Do you have the financial freedom to provide that pet with quality care? Will your living quarters allow a pet to reside there comfortably? If your answers are "yes," you are on your way to an enriched family experience.

CHAPTER SUMMARY

Points to Remember

- Before selecting your pet, consider
    Cost (both initial and ongoing)
    Size
    Breed characteristics
    Grooming and other maintenance needs
    Compatibility with your family's likes, dislikes, circumstances,
        and lifestyle
- Children should be involved in pet selection. Engage them in the search for information and review together the characteristics and needs of particular pets in which they are interested. This process is fun and may forestall impulsive selections based on children's enchantment with the animal in their latest favorite movie or cartoon or the one their friend just got.
- The final responsibility for pet selection rests with you, the parent. Talk with your veterinarian; visit the library; and check Internet resources, especially sites devoted to the particular breeds in which you are interested.
- Involve the whole family in talking about just what it will mean to have the pet in the household. How will your lives change and how will you deal with the changes?
- When choosing a particular pet, find out all you can about the animal's history, especially its prior exposure to and behavior with people in general and children in particular.

Photo by Anne Guedry

Selecting the Right Pet Checklist

√ Determine about how much of your budget can be devoted to a pet, both for the initial purchase or adoption fee and for routine maintenance and veterinary care.

√ Survey the members of your family about their pet preferences.

√ Spend time, along with your children, learning about the characteristics and needs of the animals you are considering. Discuss how your family life will be different with a particular animal.

√ Make a specific plan (including who will do what) for fitting your new pet's needs (feeding, walking, changing litter, etc.) into your daily routine.

√ Consider whether your house and yard will accommodate your pet of choice. Estimate the cost of fencing your backyard if the dog will spend time outside.

√ Consider the basics, such as size, age, and breed of dog or cat that will fit in with your family's interests.

√ Talk with one or more local veterinarians about requirements and costs for basic care.

√ Check your grocery, pet supply store, or veterinary clinic to estimate the cost of a good quality pet food.

√ Make sure the pet you acquire has been properly socialized.

Photo by Linell Champagne

CHAPTER 4

"BUT *I* FED HIM LAST NIGHT!"

The Physical and Medical Responsibilities of Pet Care

Taking care of a pet is an unending job. It's almost like caring for a human baby, with one major exception. Pets are children who *never* grow up. Unlike our human children, pets never learn to take care of themselves.

Pets don't fill their own water bowls when they are thirsty; they never drive themselves to the supermarket for food when they're hungry; and they certainly don't become financially independent and move out on their own.

Pets always need us to care for them. So before pet shopping for that new family addition, think about what pets need and who'll be responsible for fulfilling those needs.

THE BASICS: FOOD AND WATER

All pets need the basic essentials of life—food and water. This sounds so simple, but is it? Will we always be there on time to provide these essentials? Will we remember to check the water bowl every day? Will we give them the right food?

So Many Choices: What Food to Choose?

Walking down the pet food aisle can be an entertaining and mind-boggling experience. Who would ever imagine that there could be so many cat and dog foods on the market? Is there any wonder that pet food is a multibillion-dollar industry? To narrow your choices, visit your pet's nutritionist—your veterinarian. Your veterinarian will know the most appropriate diet for your dog or cat and can answer any questions you or your child may have.

Your veterinarian will explain that dogs and cats need age-appropriate diets to ensure proper growth and bone development. Also, different breeds have different nutritional needs. A Great Dane pup will not eat the same food as a Pomeranian. These different canine breeds require different formulations to grow properly. There are diets specifically made for large breeds and small breeds that balance the growth of bone, muscle, and cartilage to avoid developmental orthopedic problems. Simply feeding the correct food may help your pet avoid hip dysplasia and OCD (osteochondritis dissecans), a growth-related shoulder problem.

The size of the dog may affect the size of the kibble itself. Very small dogs may like a smaller morsel of food, and there are brands that accommodate this preference. A one-and-a-half-pound Chihuahua may have a hard time chewing a food kernel the size of a quarter.

Healthy kittens have food preferences too, but size here is not an issue. All kittens grow at about the same rate and need basically the same general diets. Since adult cat size is less variable than that of dogs, adult cat food is easier to choose, too. High-quality commercial food is a good choice for healthy cats that do not have specific dietary needs.

FOOD CONVERSION

Proper diet is crucial to the overall growth and health of both dogs and cats. If the pup or kitten is eating a good diet instituted by the breeder, the veterinarian may advise you to continue that food; however, if another diet would be more appropriate, a change may be in order. And this is just one more change added to a heap of changes experienced by a new pet, so it needs to be accomplished gradually. Not only has the young animal been taken away from his mother and siblings, he's been taken for a ride in a strange vehicle driven by strange people only to arrive at a strange place (i.e., the doctor's office or your house).

The key to uneventful food conversion is to take your time introducing the new food. For the first few days your new pet is at home, make no changes in his diet. Providing the diet has been approved by your veterinarian, feed the same food the previous owner or breeder or pet shop fed him. Then begin mixing the new food to the old in a 50:50 ratio. Increase the new food and decrease the old over a few days so that eventually the pet eats only the new food. Gradual initiation of a new diet will help prevent intestinal upsets.

Puppies, kittens, and adult pets alike should be fed a food that is highly digestible. A premium food will mean more is digested and utilized while less is eliminated. Sounds good, right?

It bears repeating—it's important that you feed only the advised diet. That means no sneaking tidbits from your plate. Feeding table food may cause intestinal upsets in your pet. You'll regret giving that puppy part of your hamburger when you have to clean up after him the next morning.

Make sure the entire family follows your veterinarian's nutritional advice. There should be no cheating allowed. Teach your children that pet food is for pets and people food is for people. This is one time that sharing is not a nice thing to do.

Feeding Schedules

Feeding schedules are important for pets of all ages but are particularly important for young pets, especially puppies. Unlike kittens who are self-regulated eaters, pups should be fed individual meals several times a day. Feeding on schedule is better for the pup's digestion, helps maintain a consistent glucose level, and facilitates housebreaking. Pups that eat on schedule are also more likely to digest and eliminate on schedule.

Puppies should be fed three times daily if possible. Put the appropriate amount of food in the bowl and allow the pup ten to fifteen minutes to consume it. Pick up any leftover food after this time to discourage between-meal snacking. Repeat the feeding process at lunch and again at dinner time.

Working couples who are not home for the lunchtime feeding can alter the schedule as follows. Feed the pup first thing in the morning, picking up the bowl after ten to fifteen minutes. Right before leaving for the day, put a second portion of food down for the pup's midday meal. The last meal should be offered at dinner time. Frequent feedings maintain adequate blood glucose levels in small pups, so timing is crucial. It's not good to be late for dinner.

Feeding is much easier for felines. Cats, unlike dogs, do well with ad-lib feeding. They will nibble their food during the day or night, usually without overeating. Like their canine friends, cats need a high-quality, digestible diet. Good food will reduce the amount of feces produced, making litter box clean up easier. Also, litter box odor is reduced when the cat is fed a high-quality diet.

During the nutrition class in your veterinarian's office or in your home, explain to your child that pet treats are a little like cookies—they taste good but aren't as healthy as a regular meal. Children need to understand that too many treats may ruin the pet's appetite and his ability or desire to consume enough of his regular food to fulfill his nutritional requirements. And the extra calories in snacks mean extra pounds on the pet.

Help your child choose good snacks for your pet. Read the labels, paying attention to calorie content. Avoid snacks with dyes in them. These may look more appealing to you, but the color of the snack doesn't mean a thing to your pet, except possibly more intestinal problems. All snacks should be approved by your pet's doctor.

The best snack is the pet's regular kibble. Simply place a measured amount of the pet's normal dry food in a small ziplock bag and allow the child to "treat" the pet at will. You can put a daily ration of the kibble in the special bag and explain to the child that the bag contains all the "treats" the dog or cat is allowed to have in a single day. This is also a good lesson in moderation for your child.

Another good snack comes from the freezer and breaks one of the cardinal pet food rules. Feeding dogs frozen vegetables breaks the no-table-food advice, but it's a good exception to the rule. A bag of frozen mixed vegetables including carrots, green beans, cauliflower, and broccoli provides a handy, healthy snack. (No onions, please.) Your child can reach in and give the pet a frozen veggie as a nutritious snack with few calories.

Water, Water Everywhere

In addition to food, dogs and cats require a constant supply of clean, fresh water. Although they need to be supervised, children can help wash, rinse, and fill water bowls. There is no restriction on the amount of water your child can give your pet, and keeping the water bowl filled can actually be a fun job for your child.

Designate a fill line on the bowl to help minimize spillage from overfilling by enthusiastic water boys and water girls. Mark the fill line on the bowl in permanent marker and instruct your young pet helper to pour water only up to that spot. This will not only decrease overflows but will allow your child a little independence.

You'll be surprised how children enjoy this responsibility. Some youngsters really take this job seriously and make countless trips per day to the water dispenser or sink. Even with an enthusiastic helper, remember to check on the water bowl daily just in case your child forgets to do his job.

Setting the Table: Finding the Best Pet Bowl

When it comes to feeding and watering pets, the utensils we use make a difference. No, the cat really doesn't need a footed crystal glass for his food as shown in the TV ad, but the dish does matter.

Obviously, glass is fragile, so it's best to avoid breakable pet bowls no matter how cute they are. Especially with children handling the bowls, the indestructible varieties are preferable.

Plastic bowls are an affordable, easy to clean, nonbreakable option, but have two disadvantages. Plastic bowls are sometimes lightweight and skid across the floor when voracious dogs gulp their food. This leads to messy mealtimes. Second, some dogs and cats are allergic to the chemicals in plastic bowls and develop skin irritations around the muzzle.

Ruling out glass and plastic puts metal bowls at the top of the list. Stainless steel bowls may be a bit pricey and may not be the prettiest dinnerware, but they are long lasting, unbreakable, hypoallergenic, and easy to clean. They also come with rubber liners on the bottoms to prevent skidding or tipping, reducing the mess associated with mealtime. For pet owners who like a designer touch, many bowls come in a variety of holders that keep them in place and look good too.

Dining Etiquette: Where Will Your Pet Eat?

In addition to the proper dishes, inside cats and dogs need to be accommodated with private dining areas. Both cats and dogs prefer to eat away from the main traffic lanes of the house. If disrupted during mealtime, pets often become agitated and may even develop intestinal disorders.

Putting the pet's food in an isolated area also reduces the chance that young toddlers will "sneak" a snack out of the pet's bowl. To a toddler, the dog's kibble may be more appealing than a chocolate chip cookie. Parents may be rightly concerned about the pet food making the child sick. While processing usually removes harmful bacteria from the food, we have learned from experience that even good pet foods can carry harmful contaminants. So, it's better to teach the child not to consume anything from bowls that lie on the floor.

You should also supervise your dog during mealtime to ensure that he consumes all the food. Lack of appetite may be the first sign of illness. Mealtime supervision shouldn't take very long if your dog is fed on schedule and has minimal between-meal snacks. He should be hungry enough to empty his bowl within minutes.

Cats are ad-lib feeders, so their food bowls almost always have kibble in them. How do you stop your toddler from accessing this temptation? Simply place the cat's food and water bowls in a location that your toddler cannot reach. Cats don't mind jumping on the clothes dryer to dine. Just be sure the dryer door remains closed.

A cat's food consumption is a little more difficult to monitor since cats eat at will. The cat should be fed a predetermined daily amount and should consume the entire portion in twenty-four hours. Feeding a measured daily ration makes food monitoring easier and more accurate.

Outside dogs and cats have mealtime considerations, too. They should have specified feeding areas just like inside pets and should be monitored for food consumption. If the pet doesn't finish his meal, you need to discard any leftover food to avoid ant and fly infestations. This may mean that ad-lib feeding cats adopt a dining schedule.

Water bowls can be located next to food bowls for inside or outside pets. Unlike food bowls that are empty between meals, water bowls should always be full. Access to fresh water should be a constant for both inside and outside pets.

THE AFTER-DINNER STROLL: LATRINE DUTY

Regardless of the type of pet you have, a toilet plan is a must. If you have a house-trained adult dog and a fenced yard, this may be as simple as letting Fido outside for a few minutes after meals and before bedtime. If you walk your dog, latrine duty needs to be more carefully scheduled.

Teaching your dog to go to a designated spot will avoid soiling areas where children play and make picking up after him easier. Picking up feces is mandatory in some communities and just plain polite when dogs are walked in public areas.

Photo by Tiffiny Clark

For a puppy just learning about toilet training, schedules are even more important. Housebreaking requires consistent adherence to a schedule for taking the puppy outside when he wakes up, after meals, before bedtime, and often at intervals in between. Intermittent outdoor walks are necessary when your pup signals you with a bark, a whimper, an approach to the door, or an intense search for just the right spot. That's a lot of going outside. Housebreaking is another of those pet-care activities that calls for advanced planning, taking into consideration when certain family members are at home. In today's busy households, it may take an entire family working together diligently to train a single pup.

Some pups cannot wait until someone comes home to let them outside. They simply have to go. Confining puppies to a crate when you are away may prevent accidents from occurring all over the house but does little to actually stop a desperate pup from "going." Try to be considerate of the pup's physical needs. That may mean forgoing all but the absolutely essential after-school or after-work errands so that you can literally "relieve" your pet.

This same consideration should be extended to older pets that may have trouble "holding it." But basically, dogs of any age need to have their elimination needs met, and the responsibility to meet those needs may have to be shared by several family members.

No matter how devoted you are to the task, you will inevitably witness housebreaking accidents. Try to minimize their impact by using doors or baby gates to confine puppies to surfaces that are easier to clean. Clean the soiled area thoroughly so that the odor doesn't encourage the animal to return to the spot the next time nature calls. Disinfecting also reduces your exposure to bacteria and parasites.

Remember that punishing dogs after the fact for housebreaking accidents (or for anything else) has no effect except to confuse them and make them afraid of you. Don't fall for the old "rub their nose in it" advice. Also, resist the urge to scoop up a puppy "in the act" and rush him out the back door to finish his job. Going outside should never be punishment; it should always be a positive experience.

If you catch your pup in the act of an inappropriate elimination, put him in time-out. Time out can be any area of the house that is private and isn't used for pet eating or sleeping. When in time out, your pet does not receive any attention from you. Withholding attention is negative reinforcement of inappropriate acts. Time-out sessions should be limited to just a minute or two. In fact, simply placing your pet in time out, instructing him to sit, and turning your back on him may be all that is necessary. And remember to really praise your puppy whenever he eliminates outside so he understands what positive reinforcement and loving attention is.

LITTER BOX DUTY: THE GREAT EQUALIZER

Kittens don't pose a big housebreaking dilemma and are usually easy to litter train. They generally grasp the notion fairly quickly if they are taken to a clean litter pan after they are fed. Find a place for kitty's toilet that is out of the way but easy to access, change the litter frequently, and you should have no trouble housebreaking your kitten.

It's best to locate the litter box in a quite area of the house that provides privacy for the cat. Some cats simply will not use the litter box if it is in a high-traffic area. Besides, most cat owners prefer to locate litter boxes in restricted areas. Who wants to see or smell a litter box? Of course, you shouldn't put the litter box so far off the beaten path that it's inconvenient for the cat and you forget to clean it. Out of sight (and smell), out of mind?

Avoid enclosed litter pans that may also make it easier for you to overlook the need to clean them. Enclosed litter pans don't just conceal the excrement, they hold in odors. Cats don't like using a poorly ventilated, foul-smelling restroom any more than you do.

It may be best to put litter box cleaning on the family schedule to make sure it gets done regularly. Litter boxes are going to get nasty, but they are easier to clean when you provide two things: a high-quality digestible diet that reduces the amount of fecal output and is healthier for the cat, and unscented, low-dust litter that clumps when wet. Cats usually do not appreciate perfumed litter as much as their human housemates, and human housemates usually do not like the manner in which cats communicate their dislike for a particular litter, so try to get it right the first time.

If you have any questions or concerns about house-training methods for your pup or kitten, consult your veterinarian for advice right away. The sooner you get it right, the sooner your pet will too. Also, with any pet, report changes in elimination habits that could indicate a medical problem. Some cats are prone to urinary infections and blockages that can become serious, even fatal, if not treated early. So watch for changes in the frequency with which your cat visits the litter box, signs of straining to urinate, or blood in the urine.

EXERCISE FOR HEALTH

Part of keeping a dog healthy is keeping him physically fit. That means not only feeding him the proper diet and providing clean water but also enabling him to get the proper amount of physical activity. The degree of physical activity required varies with the breed of dog.

Active herding breeds, sight dogs, hunting dogs, and retrievers need lots of physical activity. They are not content to lounge all day in their house or in yours. They want to GO! And you need to have the time to go with them. But, not just energetic dogs need exercise. Even more sedate breeds need a good physical workout. In fact, all dogs in reasonable health should exercise a little each day with longer walks two or three times a week.

Finding time to exercise this much with your pet is difficult for busy parents, but it's worth the effort. Coordinated exercise benefits you *and* the dog. The bond between you and your dog grows as you spend time together, plus you both get a good workout. And an exercised dog is usually less hyperactive and more controllable at home.

Families can work exercise into the family routine with a little forethought. When you walk to the mailbox, take the dog along. When you borrow milk from the neighbor, take the dog along. When you take the baby out for a stroll, take the dog along. Who says you have to walk two miles all at one time?

Leash training is critical when walking the dog. Having a dog braid the leash around the stroller wheels or tangle it around your feet while you're carrying an armload of mail or a quart of milk is no fun and can be dangerous.

A leash-trained dog is a pleasure to take along for long or short walks and the dog feels included in the daily routine. Plus, walking the dog and the baby together further solidifies the dog's position in the family and reduces the "left out" feeling some dogs have as parents become focused on the children.

A Walk in the Park: Dog Park Etiquette and Safety

For urban dwellers without big backyards or open neighborhoods, it's a good idea to look into parks that are dog friendly. You can enjoy the outdoors and exercise with your dog and the children at the same time.

Many cities have designated dog parks that provide excellent places for dogs to exercise, but these aren't always ideal spots for families with children. Be aware that in dog parks, canines are often allowed off-leash. Imagine the chaos of twenty dogs running freely in an acre of grassy area. Parents need to be careful when bringing children along to dog parks. Not all these dogs running free are accustomed to children. Have your child close to you at all times. Here's a good opportunity to teach the "ask before you pet a strange dog" rule.

To minimize the chaos and to increase safety, your dog should be voice controlled before you venture to a dog park. You should be confident that your dog will come when called even if he is flirting with a cute canine. More importantly, your dog should come on command when he meets the *other* dog who is flirting with the same cutie. No fighting over girls should be allowed.

Wise dog owners will also observe the behavior of other dogs before allowing their pet off-leash in a dog park. If you see signs that indicate aggression (hair raised, growling, or ears forward) in other dogs in the park, be forewarned, and keep your dog out until the problem dog leaves or return at another time.

Dogs at parks are like children at daycare—they are exposed to things that they don't encounter at home. In an effort to minimize exposure to infectious diseases, well-managed dog parks will encourage pet owners to keep the pet's immunizations updated, but this request may not be stringently enforced. There will be no doggie attendant policing the area asking to see vaccination verifications. Be smart! Before visiting the dog park, make sure your dog is fully protected against contagious diseases—especially kennel cough, which spreads easily between dogs playing together.

Dogs will also leave a few things behind when visiting parks—things like fleas, ticks, and intestinal worms. Examine your dog closely for fleas and ticks after each visit to the park and treat accordingly. You don't want to bring these pests home with you.

You also don't want to leave any fragrant evidence of your dog's visit to the park. It's polite to pick up after your dog if he just can't wait to get home to go to the bathroom. Contamination of an enclosed area by parasite-laden feces increases exposure to intestinal parasites exponentially. Give your dog year-round preventive medication for intestinal parasites to prevent infestations from exposure at parks.

Catwalks Really Are Scary

When it comes to cats, don't expect to find a kitty park. And don't expect cats to relish the idea of walking around the block with you either. Face it—cats don't look up at you with expectant eyes eager to go for a jog. You have to exercise a little creativity to exercise a cat.

Fooling a cat is not easy, but perhaps you can disguise exercise time to look like play time, *if* you can get your cat to play. Since many cats are happy just to lie in the windowsill all day, they may need a little coaxing to exercise, such as being entertained with a cute cat toy. There are many safe, fun feline toys that may lure your cat into physical activity.

Enough about walking and visiting parks. What about a little downtime at home? Pets stay at home for several reasons. First, they can't drive themselves around in a car, so they depend on you to take them out. Second, pets are safer at home than they are traipsing around town on foot exposed to other animals or walking in the path of a vehicle. Third, many communities have laws governing pet confinement.

In many communities, dogs and cats are required to stay indoors unless they are in a fenced in yard or are on a leash being walked by their owners. There are fines attached to infractions of municipal ordinances regulating pet confinement. And many pets end up at the pound when they are found wandering around without their owners in tow.

Keeping a pet securely at home means either keeping him indoors or safely confining him outdoors; therefore, fencing the yard may be a big part of your pet-owning responsibility. There are two options for fencing the yard—traditional fencing or underground electronic fencing. Both have advantages and disadvantages.

Traditional versus Electronic Fencing

Traditional fences (wood or metal) prevent dogs from entering or exiting your yard. Your dog won't be able to get out and other dogs won't be able to get in. Electronic fences or perimeter guards may keep *your* dog in the yard but will not keep *other* dogs out.

Electronic devices will, therefore, not eliminate your dog's exposure to diseases and parasites carried by visiting dogs, nor will they prevent dog fights. In fact, fights may erupt as your dog tries to defend his territory against the trespasser. And your dog will think it highly unfair if other dogs tease him just beyond the borders of the electronic fence.

But electronic fences also have advantages. They are often less costly than traditional fences and do not affect the yard's appearance—they truly are invisible. Most dogs are easily trained to respect the boundaries of the invisible fence and wear a special battery-operated collar that provides a gentle reminder should they forget those boundaries. Electric fences require an active battery-operated collar to be effective. Batteries need to be replaced three or four times a year. Many electric fence companies encourage owners to join a membership program that automatically sends a new battery at appropriate intervals. Other types of electronic devices or perimeter guards need upkeep too.

"Born Free": How to Confine a Cat

Outside cats cannot effectively be contained by either electronic or traditional fences unless the yard has a net or fence ceiling. Outside cats are essentially free-roaming creatures. They can scale fences and run free. This means that cats that roam or are visited by other roaming cats have an increased exposure to parasites and infectious diseases. Some of these diseases, such as feline immunodeficiency virus (FIV) and feline leukemia virus (FeLV) can be life threatening.

Car-related injuries also shorten the lives of many free-roaming outside cats. Add to that the possibility of the infamous cat fight and you have plenty of reasons to keep your cat indoors.

A Room with a View—And a Few Amenities

Dogs that live outside need more than just a fence. They also need protective shelter. Exposure to inclement weather, whether extreme cold, heat, or precipitation, is a safety hazard, so unless you have a big covered porch or an accessible canine area in the garage, plan to build or purchase a dog kennel.

Commercial doghouses made of durable, easy-to-clean materials come in many sizes and styles. If you build a wooden doghouse, lift it off the ground to retard rotting and paint it with nontoxic paint or sealant. Make sure the products are not toxic because your dog may love his house enough to eat it.

Where you place the doghouse in the yard requires a little thought. Your dog's house should be in an area that has adequate shade and ventilation for those hot summer months as well as protection from cold winter winds. The kennel should also be situated away from child play areas to decrease human exposure to intestinal parasite eggs eliminated in the dog's feces. You don't want your children playing in the dog's latrine.

As for the neighbors, think about their close proximity to your dog's humble abode. Are they so close that your dog will be a nuisance when he plays and barks? Many communities have noise ordinances to prevent excessive dog barking, and you definitely don't want to be an owner of an illegal beagle howling at the moon.

Think about the amount of time your dog will be confined to a kennel enclosure and what he will do there. How would you like to spend ten to twelve hours at a time, day after day, in one room—even a really nice room—with no form of entertainment or distraction? Sounds pretty boring doesn't it? Your dog will feel the same way, so remember to provide plenty of interesting toys to help him pass the time he must spend there. Lonely, bored dogs are prone to behavior problems.

Although it is advisable to keep your cat indoors, those that do live outside need protective shelter. Cats may adjust to an outside "doghouse," but many prefer to be close to the human house. Consider allowing your outside cat to inhabit an area of the garage or back porch. Keep fresh water available there at all times. Monitor the food bowl very closely. Cats are nibblers, not gobblers. They rarely empty the food bowl at one sitting, making the leftovers in the bowl open to invasion by ants and other animals looking for a snack.

Cats need not only a place to eat, sleep, and get out of the rain but also a protected area in which to retreat from other cats roaming the neighborhood. Fences don't keep out wandering cats, and uninvited feline guests may expose your outside cat to infectious diseases or even inflict injuries. And even though you may be comfortable leaving your cat outdoors, the birds and bird lovers in your neighborhood may object. For these reasons, many cat owners keep their kitties strictly inside the big house.

Inside the Big House

If you decide that your dog or cat will reside indoors with you, there are a few things to remember. Pets need a private area to eat and rest away from household activities. They also need a quiet place to spend the night. If they don't sleep on your bed, or couch, or rug, they need a comfortable bed of their own. And like your own bedding, it will need to be washed occasionally.

Inside pets can be taught to respect boundaries set for them. This will prevent household mishaps. Remember to be consistent in enforcing the boundaries to avoid sending mixed signals to your pet. If you allow the cat on the living room sofa but your partner doesn't, you end up with a confused kitty.

No matter what kind of fence or doghouse you have, your pet may not be completely safe, even in your very own backyard. In fact, even pets that stay inside your home may still be at risk. Each year, many pets are lost or stolen.

Pet loss can often be prevented, and, when it does occur, the animal's return can be facilitated by a few simple precautions. First, always make sure that your dog or cat has identification on its body. Identification tags are readily available at pet stores, by mail order, and at many veterinary offices. Do not delay in getting one for your pet. Even cats that are kept indoors all the time should have identification. You never know when a door might accidentally be left open and the cat might wander out. We have recently learned of a friend's loss of two cats in just this way. For cats, identification tags should be attached to break-away collars that will prevent the animal's hanging should it be caught when climbing. That, of course, will save the animal's life but cause the loss of the identification, which brings us to the next recommended precaution—microchipping.

Microchipping

Yes, the computer age has come to animals. Your pet can have a tiny microchip carrying a unique identification number inserted under its skin. This number corresponds to owner identification information that is entered into a national database.

Microchipping, which is performed in many veterinary clinics, is inexpensive, quick, safe, and virtually painless for the animal. The microchip, slightly larger than a grain of rice, is injected with a special syringe and needle just under the pet's skin. Microchipping should be done at the first opportunity. It could literally save your pet's life.

Almost all veterinary clinics and animal shelters now have policies that call for the routine scanning of stray animals to determine if they have a microchip identifier. Many owners have had their lost animals returned because they had the foresight to have them undergo this quick procedure. Newer microchips may be linked to a database including pertinent medical information about the pet. With this new technology, a lost cat with diabetes could receive the appropriate insulin or a lost dog with a seizure disorder could be given the right anticonvulsant.

Because the microchipped animal wears a tag bearing his identification number, he may also be less subject to theft. Liken a microchip ID tag to a sign outside your house announcing that you have a security system installed. The tag is a similar deterrent to theft.

Low-Tech Pet Loss Prevention

Now a word about preventing pet loss. Consider these facts: Households with children are very busy and children are not always careful. That means that gates and doors get left open and pets wander out. The straying of pets due to open gates and doors can be minimized by simple spring closures. To protect children and animals, a spring should not be so tight that it slams back with great force, but it should be sufficiently tight to close the gate or door if someone forgets to do so.

Taking pets on excursions can also create risk. Yes, it's fun to take your animal to the park. Visiting friends can also be fun (but be sure the animal is welcome there and keep it on a leash). Harnesses rather than collars add an extra measure of safety for traveling animals. A pet in a strange situation can become easily frightened and can pull out of a traditional buckled collar. Sliding leashes are a little more escape proof, but they put pressure on the dog's trachea as he pulls away. Harnesses do not choke the pet and do not slip off if they fit and are fastened correctly. Brachycephalic (short-nosed) dogs and all types of cats do particularly well with harnesses.

When taking your pet out of your yard, use common sense to protect him. Animals left in cars invite theft and, in many climates, are at serious risk of becoming fatally overheated. Summertime temperatures rise very quickly in unventilated cars, making vehicles potential death traps for pets. Never leave an unattended dog or cat in any car, even in colder weather, without extremely frequent supervision.

Traveling sounds risky but can be quite safe when certain precautions are taken, and taking pets on outings is part of the fun of pet ownership for you and for the pet. Still, you may think "there's no place like home" for you and your pet.

Think again! Particularly if your animal is purebred, think twice about leaving it in a yard that can be easily accessed from outside of your house. Be extremely cautious if you are routinely away and your comings and goings can be monitored. Unimpeded access to an animal that appears valuable can invite theft. Keep your pet safe by not making him an easy mark for a thief.

ROUTINE CARE FROM THE PROFESSIONALS

Like humans, all pets, regardless of age or health status, need routine preventive care to stay healthy. That means that pets shouldn't see the veterinarian just when they are sick.

Healthy pets need to visit the veterinarian at least once and preferably twice annually. Does this sound like a lot to you? Well, think of it this way. Dogs and cats age faster than you do. When your pet sees the veterinarian once a year, that's the equivalent of your seeing your own doctor every seven or eight years.

Routine veterinary visits should be a positive experience for the pet and the family. Let your child know that this is another regular activity for your pet. Don't make a big deal out of the trip to the doctor—it's just another part of pet care.

To desensitize your pet and your child before the veterinary visit, take them both on frequent car rides that end somewhere besides the veterinary hospital. Make these outings fun by stopping by a park for play time. That way the pet and the child won't associate getting in the car with going to the veterinarian.

The White Coat Syndrome

Veterinarians fully understand the "white coat syndrome." Seeing a grown-up in a white lab coat puts dread into the hearts of pets and children alike. Children are often afraid of veterinarians as much as pets are because they fear the white lab coat. After all, the other person they see in a lab coat often has a needle in his hand aimed right at them.

Find a veterinarian who will take time to establish a rapport with your child. Veterinarians usually enjoy seeing children and welcome their participation in routine pet care visits. A calm conversation and a small treat for both the pet and the child will make the visit more than bearable. The right doctor may even make it enjoyable.

Veterinarians take children seriously and want to include them in pet care. Doctors realize that when they communicate well with children, they are essentially educating the next generation of pet owners.

Well-health veterinary visits will start with a complete physical examination. Children relate to the pet's exam by recalling their own physicals. They usually understand and identify with the "ins and outs" of a physical. They recognize that some things go in (thermometers, otoscopes) and other things come out (blood and other "samples"). They quickly realize that the pet's doctor does many of the same things their pediatrician does.

Pets, like very young children, cannot communicate on their own, making examination and diagnosis all the more challenging for the doctor. When your pet has a physical exam, the doctor will take its temperature; examine the eyes, ears, nose, mouth, and teeth; listen to the heart and lungs; palpate (feel) the abdomen and lymph nodes; survey the coat; and check for lameness. Ask your doctor to explain what he's doing as he examines your pet.

Children watch the examination process with rapt attention. They especially enjoy listening to the pet's heartbeat and comparing the rate with their own. (The dog or cat will have a faster heart rate.) Ask your doctor for this opportunity and he'll likely be happy to share his stethoscope for a minute or two.

Only so much can be learned from an external physical examination, so your veterinarian may perform other tests. She will check the pet's stool for intestinal parasites. (If you bring in a stool sample in a plastic bag, this endeavor will be a little less pleasant for you, but a lot more pleasant for your pet.)

He will also perform blood tests, checking the dog's blood for heartworms and tick-borne diseases. The doctor may check your cat's blood for contagious viral diseases including FIV and FeLV and for heartworms, too. He may perform additional blood work and a urinalysis on your pet to evaluate major organ function.

Although twice-yearly medical visits are the norm for adult dogs and cats, young animals see the veterinarian monthly as they go through an initial series of immunizations necessary to protect them from a variety of contagious diseases. They will be dewormed often to protect them and their owners from intestinal parasites. (We cover this in detail in chapter 6.)

Immunizations are an important part of a pet's well-health care even beyond puppy and kitten time. Booster vaccinations are necessary to maintain an adequate level of immunity against contagious diseases. The types and frequency of vaccinations will be determined by your pet's doctor. Commonly administered vaccinations, some of which are combined in a single injection, include, for dogs: distemper, hepatitis, leptospirosis, parainfluenza, bordetella, Lyme disease, parvovirus, and rabies; for cats: feline viral rhinotracheitis, calicivirus, panleukopenia, feline leukemia virus, feline immunodeficiency virus, and rabies. There is also a vaccine for dogs that are susceptible to periodontal disease. With such a wide array of potential vaccines it's best to speak to your veterinarian about which immunizations are necessary for your dog or cat.

Spaying and Neutering

Young cats and dogs will also have an extra visit to the doctor for reproductive management. If your new pet is still unnueutered, you should discuss this matter with your veterinarian on the very first visit. Both male and female animals that are not breeding pets should be neutered, but the surgical procedures differ. When female dogs and cats are neutered, an abdominal incision is made and the uterus and both ovaries are removed (called ovariohysterectomy). When males are neutered, the testicles are removed (called castration) with a more superficial incision outside the abdominal wall unless one or both testicles are retained within the abdomen. Even though these procedures are referred to as routine, remember that there is no such thing as *routine* surgery. So find a doctor you trust.

Since most veterinary hospitals perform these procedures, many pet owners shop around for the best price on reproductive surgery. Take heed and compare prices carefully. Make sure the fee includes everything involved in the procedure (pre-op lab work, anesthesia, anesthetic monitoring, surgery, hospitalization, pain management, antibiotics). The least expensive choice may not be the best one.

With the special needs of young pets, prepare to spend more time and money at the veterinary clinic in the beginning. After the first year, visits level out. But remember, these routine veterinary visits will keep your pet on the right path to a long, healthy life.

WHEN THE VETERINARY VISIT ISN'T ROUTINE

The number and frequency of veterinary visits are not so routine for ill or aged pets. These dogs and cats have special needs that require more intense medical attention and they may develop a problem that cannot wait until the next scheduled visit. Old pets or pets with medical problems place an increased demand on a family's time and budget.

Older and ill pets may undergo more diagnostic evaluations on these veterinary visits in order for the doctor to monitor their aging or malfunctioning organs. Blood work and urine tests are very useful tools, but more in-depth diagnostics, including ultrasounds, radiographs, and ECGs, may be performed as needed. These diagnostics are not invasive and involve minimal, if any, discomfort for your dog or cat.

Using these more advanced techniques provides early diagnoses and accurate assessment of medical problems. Early diagnosis means early treatment, and accurate assessment means accurate treatment. Both mean better care and a longer life span for dogs and cats.

But, good medical care can also mean a greater expenditure of time and money on the family's part. If you have a young pet, eventually you will (hopefully) have an older pet, so make sure you are prepared to provide medical care for that pet throughout his life.

Veterinary visits can be frequent and complicated, so although children may certainly want to accompany you, medical care should be the responsibility of an adult. Parents cannot expect a young child to make medical appointments or comprehend medical jargon. Adults need to take charge of a pet's medical care but include the child in a way that matches her age, temperament, individual sensibilities, and practical circumstances.

Hospital Stays Are Scary

Sometimes, pets need to stay overnight in the hospital. Some surgical procedures and illnesses require hospitalization. If your pet has to stay in the hospital, you may need to comfort the pet *and* the child. Explain to the child that the hospital stay is in the pet's best interest and that the hospital staff will do their best to make him feel at home and comfortable.

Leave the pet's favorite toy or blanket with him at the hospital. This will make the pet and the child feel more comfortable and may decrease the pet's sense of abandonment. Put your name on each article you leave at the veterinary clinic to facilitate return of your pet's things. Do you really think that your blue towel is the *only* blue towel in the hospital?

Allow your child to visit the pet during the hospitalization to see for himself that his furry friend is in good hands. Prepare the child for the pet's condition. If your pet will be bandaged or have stitches or will be hooked up to an IV, explain this to your child *before* the visit. Decrease the shock potential with adequate preparation. This will also decrease the fear factor associated with hospital stays.

Expect the Unexpected: Unanticipated Responsibilities

You may think you know full well what pet care responsibilities lay ahead of you, but there may be a surprise lurking just around the corner. Pets are unpredictable and accidents do happen. So it's best to anticipate some of the more common emergency-room situations.

Children and pets interacting together are an accident waiting to happen. Cats will try to climb too high and fall down. Puppies will rush out the back door behind a child and get crunched in the process. Children will accidentally stick their fingers into wide-open dog and cat eyes. What do you do when the unexpected occurs? Is there a pet 911?

Actually, there is a pet emergency number—you just need to find out what it is. Ask your veterinarian what to do in case of an emergency. Does he handle his own emergency calls? Does he refer them to a twenty-four-hour emergency hospital?

If your veterinarian assigns after-hours call to another facility, where is it? You don't want to be scrambling through town lost with a crying puppy and a crying child in the backseat. It's best to map out the route to the emergency clinic and have the directions filed right beside the hospital's phone number. It's also a good idea to drive by the clinic before an emergency occurs so that you are familiar with the neighborhood and can recognize the building. Remember—you will likely be looking for it in the dark.

Call the emergency clinic prior to driving off in the car. The attending doctor will advise you of any actions you should take at home. Quick at-home emergency care, such as hemorrhage control, could save your pet's life. And calling ahead gives the attending doctor time to prepare for your arrival.

CLEANING AND GROOMING

Thankfully, life with a pet is not always an adrenaline rush caused by an emergency. Many ordinary tasks are associated with keeping a pet healthy. One such task is keeping the pet clean. Hopefully, you considered this responsibility as you decided what type of pet to get. Remember the long hair versus short hair question in your family survey? Well, long- and even short-haired cats and dogs need a little help staying clean and this can be a real family affair.

Keeping the pet clean can be less mundane and more fun if you make it an event. Call bath time a day at the spa. Get your gear in order—brush, nail trimmers, shampoo, towels, relaxing drink (for you, not the dog).

Brushing and Bathing

Start the pet's spa day by brushing loose hair from the dog or cat. Begin by brushing the fur in the direction of hair growth, then brush back against the grain. Try to work out stubborn knots with your fingers or carefully cut them out with grooming scissors. Yanking at knots can irritate the pet's skin and is painful.

Frequent brushing between spa days will decrease the formation of matted fur. Mats can be uncomfortable for the pet and often lead to skin infections called "hot spots," so detangling your cat or dog is important. Also, it's far better to brush the fur off the pet at one time in one area than to clean up hair shed all over the house all the time.

After brushing the coat, it's time to bathe your dog or cat. Bathing can be a fun time or a miserable time. It's what you make of it. Approach the pet cautiously, but confidently. Have the pet restrained by a leash in case he becomes too excited and tries to escape his spa treatment.

Cats are great escape artists when presented for a bath, so be on guard. Cats also have a noted aversion to water and they do not like to be splashed. It's better to wet them by pouring water over them from a pitcher as opposed to using a hose or sprayer. Pouring water is also quieter. The sound of a high-pressure hose is disconcerting for cats.

Dogs, on the other hand, may not mind the water hose. In fact, they often want to play with the water. That makes getting them saturated a little difficult, but getting yourself saturated rather easy.

Once the dog or cat is thoroughly wet, lather the waterlogged pet with

Photo by Linell Champagne

shampoo, getting the suds all the way to the skin. Avoid getting shampoo in the pet's eyes. Shampoo in the eyes is uncomfortable and can even cause eye injuries such as corneal abrasions. Prior to the bath, you may want to apply mineral oil or ophthalmic ointment to protect the eyes, especially if you have a brachycephalic (short-nosed) pet such as a Pekingese or bulldog or a Persian cat. Do not use human eye preparations in your pets' eyes without consulting your veterinarian.

The pet stores shelves are lined with a confusing array of shampoos. Choose a basic hypoallergenic, moisturizing shampoo unless your pet has a skin condition that requires a medicated shampoo. If your veterinarian prescribes a medicated shampoo, bath time may be extended. Medicated shampoos only work while they are in contact with the skin, so the pet needs to soak with the suds on him. Fortunately, sudsy, soaking pets do not have to remain confined in the bath tub. They can be walked on a warm, sunny day while soaking in the shampoo.

Thorough rinsing is the next step, followed by towel drying. A blow-dryer can expedite the drying process, but should be used cautiously. Electric dryers can become hot enough to injure tender skin, and some animals may be frightened by the noise of a dryer. Hold the blow-dryer away from your pet, turn it on, and gradually move it closer.

Of course, the final step in the spa day occurs when the freshly washed pet wallows in the first available mud puddle.

FREQUENCY OF SPA DAYS

For dogs with healthy coats, monthly baths are sufficient. More frequent bathing to reduce the doggie smell can be performed as needed; however, it's best not to bathe your dog more than once a week since overbathing can dry out the coat. There are pet perfumes available to decrease the doggy odor between baths.

Persistent foul odor in an animal that is reasonably clean may signal a medical problem such as impacted anal glands, infected ears, or periodontal disease and should be evaluated by your veterinarian.

Cats are pretty good about keeping themselves clean, so they don't have to be bathed on a particular schedule unless they have dermatological problems. And cats don't get as dirty as dogs. When's the last time you saw a cat roll around in a mud puddle?

GOING TO A "REAL" SPA

No matter how good you are at brushing and bathing, some dogs and some cats need professional grooming. The frequency of grooming will vary with the breed and with the preference of the pet owner. If you can't stand to see your miniature poodle with a scruffy face or your Maltese with a long topknot, expect to visit the groomer every four to six weeks. Cats may require occasional grooming, too, but usually don't take as many trips to the spa as their canine friends.

Many families choose short-coated dogs and cats that require significantly less professional upkeep. But "less" upkeep doesn't equal "no" upkeep. Short-haired pets still need to be bathed and combed. Even the most fastidious dog or cat needs an occasional spa treatment whether it be at home or with a professional groomer.

Home grooming means spending less money, but spending more time. Professional groomers relieve you of the work, but are an added expense. So consider the time *and* money it takes to keep your pet looking good.

We love fluffy dogs and cats—we just wish they'd keep all that fluff on their bodies. It's a sad fact that all dogs and cats shed. Pets with long hair, short hair, curly hair, straight hair—they all shed.

Shedding is such a pain that it is a frequently cited reason for pet relinquishment. Home owners become frustrated with the amount of fur on furniture and bedding. How embarrassing to have your guests get up from the sofa with furry pants. Some of us even resort to purchasing furniture in a color that matches our pets so the shedding will be less obvious. But obvious or not, *the hair is there.*

There is no easy solution to the shedding dilemma. Contrary to promising advertisements, no nutraceutical or vitamin will magically eliminate shedding. All hair follicles release the hair shaft at a certain stage of normal hair development. So as hairs age, they fall out and new ones replace them.

We can't stop the hair development cycle; however, we can reduce shedding with a little work. A lustrous, healthy coat will shed less than a dry, unhealthy coat, so ask your veterinarian for advice on keeping your pet's coat healthy. Dogs and cats come in a variety of coat types and veterinarians have good advice on handling each one.

And since all hairs will eventually fall out, it's easier when we coordinate the shedding. Brushing your pet will help remove older hairs at one time, in one place. Brushing alone can reduce the amount of shedding that occurs throughout your home.

CHAPTER SUMMARY

Points to Remember

- Both dogs and cats need fresh water and nutritious food. Diets vary with age, breed, and health status, so consult a veterinarian before shopping for pet food.

- Snacks are fine as long as they are nutritious and are given in moderation. Too much snacking can lead to weight gain and malnutrition.
- Make a safe, comfortable home for your pet, both inside and out. Fence the yard and provide adequate shelter for outdoor dogs.
- If you do not have a readily available space to exercise your dog, investigate local dog parks.
- Microchip your pet as a means of permanent identification that may facilitate his return should he get lost.
- Healthy pets should visit the veterinarian twice a year. Pets with medical problems may need to see the doctor more often.
- Find a veterinarian who will interact in a positive manner with your pet and your child.
- Know in advance how your pet's doctor handles emergency calls.
- If a hospital stay is necessary, try to make the pet and the child as comfortable as possible with the situation. Have your child select a favorite toy or blanket to leave with the pet in the hospital. Be sure the item is labeled with your name and the pet's.
- Frequent brushing and bathing will help the pet maintain a healthy coat and reduce household shedding. Some pets require professional grooming.

Physical and Medical Needs Checklist

√ Ask your veterinarian any questions you may have about immunizations, deworming, and microchipping.

√ Talk with your veterinarian about any questions related to house-training, feeding, and exercising.

√ Prepare for an emergency by finding out how your veterinarian handles after-hours emergencies; learning directions to the emergency clinic if different from your veterinarian's office; posting emergency phone numbers in an easy-to-find place.

√ Establish a specific daily schedule for feeding and walking and determine where these activities will take place.

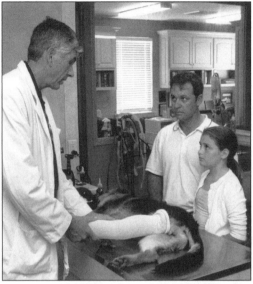

Photo by Linell Champagne

√ Make a schedule for intermittent bathing and grooming.
√ Assign duties to family members and supervise children who assist with pet care.

Photo by Linell Champagne

CHAPTER 5

LIVING, LEARNING, AND GROWING TOGETHER

Managing Child-Pet Interactions

Now that you have a cat or dog, you are no doubt looking forward to watching your children and their new companion play together and generally enjoy one another's company. You may also be wondering if there are some particular steps you might take to get your family's relationship with this new creature off to a good start and to nurture that relationship as time goes on. Indeed, there are.

GETTING STARTED

Children and pets may be meant for each other, but it cannot be assumed that children, especially young ones, know how to interact with animals. They will learn more quickly and safely if you, the parent, demonstrate appropriate handling of and interaction with the pet and encourage them to learn about and respect the animal.

All animals—dogs, cats, and so on—share certain characteristics with others of their species. But because each animal is also unique, you will need to know your new pet as an individual so that you can help your children learn to read its behavioral cues. Many factors will influence child-animal interaction. They include the type and age of the pet, its individual characteristics, children's age and temperament, their experiences with animals, and the example that you set.

As a parent, your first concern, especially if you have acquired an interactive animal such as a dog, cat, or ferret, may be about ensuring your children's safety with the animal. If you have started with an animal that has been bred and socialized to interact with children (see chapter 3), the best way to keep your children safe and to promote their enjoyment of the new pet is probably to focus first on the safety and comfort of the animal. Safe and happy child-pet relationships are not just about managing pet behavior; they can have even more to do with how children react toward pets.

Some observational study of young children with dogs has shown that the child may be more likely to treat the animal roughly than the other way around.[1] Unless you, the parent, intervene to prevent such treatment, it might eventually provoke even a good-natured animal to a defensive response. Consistent rough treatment can lead to a fearful animal and fear can trigger aggression.

Here are some simple rules that will ensure that your new pet feels safe and comfortable and is, therefore, a better playmate for your children.

A PRIVATE GETAWAY

Who doesn't need a space of his own and some protected quiet time? Even though *you* may not get much of either as a parent, your household will be a happier one if you provide them for your pet. Baby animals especially need some downtime, but all pets require a break from play and handling.

For dogs, their best special place may be a crate, as long as it is large enough for them to turn around and is comfortably furnished with a mat and a few chew toys. Once your dog becomes accustomed to a crate, he will probably go to it voluntarily when he needs a break. Under those circumstances, it is not even necessary to close the door as long as the children know that going to the crate is Fido's signal that he needs a nap. Consider the crate to be the dog's bedroom or quiet retreat area.

Cats might prefer an out-of-the-way hiding place or cubby hole. Any space that is safe and comfortable will suffice. The key point is that children understand that it is a place where Fluffy goes to rest and be quite for a while. Cats usually like to change their favorite hideaways from time to time. Kittens are likely to be out and about whenever they think it's play time; older cats may stay tucked away for a while, even when they wouldn't mind a little petting or lap sitting. This can be confusing for children, but with a little coaching, they can learn to understand that it's best not to bother Fluffy for at least a while when she leaves them to hide under the sofa or curl up in another out-of-the-way place.

Of course you want your child to have a real relationship with your pet. That's one reason you got it, right? But what kind of interaction should you expect? Children's age is a key determinant of both the character and intensity of their relationship with a companion animal.

First, it is important to understand that all young children will need instruction and supervision to interact safely with their pet. A small child may not understand that animals feel pain and can be hurt just as they can. Children may also inadvertently harm a pet in play or through activities that the child perceives as nurturing. One of us recalls when, as a six-year-old, she placed her parakeet's cage in front of the air conditioner on a particularly hot day thinking, of course, that it would feel as good to the bird as it did to her. By the time her mom came into the room and saw where Pretty Boy was, the bird had become too chilled and soon died. It is normal for children to make such assumptions. But just as tropical birds can't tolerate air that's too cool, your cat won't enjoy wading in the kiddy pool nearly as much as your three-year-old thinks she will, nor will she benefit from being rubbed down with that suntan lotion that smells and feels *sooo* good, and sharing the chocolate birthday cake with Fido could be a prelude to a veterinary emergency or worse. These cautions go for almost all children younger than ten. Now let's look a bit more closely at what you might expect of children at different stages of development.

Infants and Toddlers

An infant may not have the capacity to develop a deep bond with the pet, but may have a relationship, nonetheless. Boris Levinson, one of the first people to make scholarly observations about the child-pet relationship, noted that even infants can enjoy the tactile stimulation they receive from touching an animal, and that following a pet can encourage crawling, reaching, and walking.[2]

Generally speaking, as the child grows, so does the child-pet relationship. Toddlers who are more mobile will interact with pets on a different level than infants who are relatively stationary. They will also expect animals to adhere to the same restrictions that are set for them as children.[3] So don't be surprised when Fluffy's small owner orders her to the corner for grabbing a piece of food out of her little hand.

As we have said repeatedly, children at these ages should not be left alone with any animal, and parents should be aware of the need to give the pet a break from reaching, pulling, and chasing behaviors that the child is too young to control. This may be the stage at which Fido or Fluffy will prefer to spend more time in the crate, yard, or another room of the house.

Preschoolers

As young children move out of toddler-hood and become more social, they begin to look on pets as peers, much as they do siblings. They talk to their pets and are likely to believe that their pets understand them.[4] This means that pets can serve in a real way as both playmates and confidants. That seems to be particularly the case for an only child and for the youngest child in the household, but may be true for any child.

Children of this age can begin to help with animal care-giving tasks, and allowing them to do so can strengthen their bond with their pet and give them a sense of competency. It is especially important to supervise children's play with their pets early on. Help them practice the proper way to approach and hold the animal and to practice being gentle. Preschoolers are impulsive and don't necessarily think ahead to possible consequences. Engage them in talk about what might happen if they are too rough or if their behavior frightens the animal.

Elementary-School Children

Children of elementary school age appear to have the most involvement with their pets. Studies indicate that these are peak years for children owning and caring for their companion animals.[5] Such a finding is not surprising given that younger school-age children are old enough to participate in pet care and to independently involve pets in their activities but have not yet gained sufficient independence to spend much time away from home other than to attend school or child care.

Children of this age continue to confide in their pets, but will develop greater understanding of their pets' limitations related to language. However, they also become more aware of the sometimes negative consequences of confiding in people (reprimands from parents, teasing or gossiping by their peers), and are thus more inclined to share their innermost thoughts with the trusted (and silent) four-legged members of their family.[6]

Photo by Lynn Buzhardt

Photo by Lynn Buzhardt

Pets also may serve to extend the social networks of these children. Grade schoolers are old enough to be accorded some independence in their selection of activities and associates, and those children who have companion animals that are perceived as friendly and fun may be more attractive as playmates. Conversation may also come more easily over the head of a golden retriever or a cuddly cat than it does between two unacquainted youngsters without pets.

Teens

Adolescents continue to have a bond with their pets and consider them important. These older children may be more focused on their responsibility for and activities with their pets as well as the pet's value in enhancing social interaction with other youngsters. There is also evidence that adolescents continue to confide in their pets.[7]

This is also the time at which youngsters begin to become more interested in spending time with friends and in activities that necessitate their being away from home for longer periods. Thus it is not surprising that some studies of children's relationships with their companion animals show that pet ownership and involvement declines somewhat during the teen years.[8]

Older adolescents may also pull back a bit in their relationships with pets, anticipating that they will soon be leaving home for college or work. Youngsters of this age may feel embarrassed about acknowledging the sadness they feel at the thought of separating from a pet. Parents can help teens by acknowledging this as normal and even supporting the youth in planning how the void in that relationship might be filled for both him and the animal when he leaves. One thoughtful parent we know encouraged her older son who was about to leave for college to request that his younger brother assume the status of "official foster parent" of his German shepherd. The younger brother was honored to be asked and the older one felt better about having made a plan that provided his dog with a special connection to someone in the family. There may not be a younger sibling in your family ready to take on the major responsibility for pet care, but you can still help your teen by talking with him openly about how a pet might be affected by his departure and what can be done to make the transition as easy as possible for him, the pet, and the entire family.

MANAGING PET BEHAVIOR

So you have taught your children about respecting their pet, and giving it some quiet time. Is that all you need to do to ensure a harmonious child-pet relationship? Perhaps so, but probably not. Some relationship problems are inevitable whether the bond is between two people or between a person and a pet.

Dogs

First, let's focus on dogs. Preventing problems can be easier if the dog is properly obedience trained. This is usually best accomplished by taking (not sending) your animal to a basic obedience class with a reputable instructor. If your child is of school age, consider having him take the dog to obedience school. It can provide an opportunity for your child to develop new competencies and a stronger bond with his pet. If you do not know of an instructor, your veterinarian can probably make a recommendation. It is also a good idea to ask a trainer for references to be sure that other dog owners have had good outcomes with their animals. Most states do not license trainers, so quality and methods vary considerably. The Certification Council for Professional Dog Trainers offers testing and certification. Trainers holding this credential will use the initials CPDT (certified pet dog trainer) after their names.[9] Avoid trainers who rely on harsh correction; teaching a dog what he should do yields much better results than punishing him for doing wrong.

Even with obedience training, problems can occur with dogs. Every year in the United States, approximately four hundred thousand children sustain dog bites.[10] Most often, this is not because a dog is inherently mean, but because the child either deliberately or unwittingly does something that the dog interprets as threatening. As a parent, there are particular behaviors you should caution your children about in relation to dogs.

First, remember that even your Yorkshire terrier or miniature poodle thinks of herself as a wolf. She is a pack animal, and you and your family are her pack. Packs have hierarchy. Most (although not all) dogs readily accept that the adults in the household have higher status in the pack and thus refrain from challenges to Mom and Dad. However, the dog may not be so clear about its status in relation to the children, especially little ones. If the dog sees the children as equals or inferiors in the pack, she is likely to challenge any behavior she interprets as threatening, not only to her physical safety but also to her control of her food and possessions or to her own perceived status in the group.

Teach your children to avoid activities that may contribute to your dog's thinking that it is higher in the family pecking order or in competition with them. These include chasing the animal, disturbing its food, and, yes, even the ever-popular games of tug-of-war and keep-away. Suggest instead that they teach the animal to play fetch, using a ball, a toy, or a Frisbee, depending upon the dog's preference. Older children may be able to learn dog agility training and participate in agility trials in their communities. Teaching basic obedience and special tricks can also be a fun and healthy way for children to interact with their dog. There are many good training instruction books. And some communities have dog obedience groups that are ongoing and provide members with an opportunity to share skills and socialize their dogs together.

Many dogs, especially those beyond puppyhood, also enjoy quieter association with children. Children can learn dog massage. Dogs can also provide an uncritical yet attentive audience for children's reading practice and are, in fact, used for that purpose in some school programs.[11]

Cats

Managing cats is easier in some ways, but more difficult in others. Cats are smaller than most dogs, but they come with formidable weaponry, so it is important that you help your children learn to avoid the kinds of play or handling that may result in painful scratches. Children should not try to hold a cat that is frightened or bring it into a situation that is potentially frightening. Sometimes cats become tired of a child's company and react by scratching. Face it, a cat can be expected to tolerate only so many changes of clothing in one day. And cats with a fashion sense may object aesthetically to some of the doll clothes they're forced to wear.

Virtually no cat wants to be continuously held, chased about the house all the time, or placed near equipment (e.g., a vacuum cleaner) that creates loud noises. But to some extent, predicting what is frightening requires getting to know your individual cat. Some cats, for example, are fine with strangers who come to the home; another may be terrified when your five-year-old carries her to meet a visitor and inflict painful scratches in trying to escape.

Parents should teach children that cats will scratch, sometimes even without intending to inflict harm. Kittens that are "loved" a little too aggressively may scratch in an attempt to escape the overabundance of affection poured out by a young child.

Many parents wonder whether cats should be declawed, both to protect children and to prevent destructive behavior such as clawing furniture. Cats can usually be managed well in the household without declawing if children learn proper handling of the animal and it is provided with materials that are acceptable for scratching. In some instances, it may be necessary to block a cat's access to certain areas of the house or to teach it to stay away from those areas (see chapter 1). Cats' claws can also be trimmed, and soft caps (Soft Paws) are available that can cover the claws for several weeks before needing to be replaced. If you do decide to consider declawing, question your veterinarian carefully about the process, what to expect, and the follow-up care your cat will require. Declawing is a more radical procedure than you might think.

Behavior Specialists

Thankfully, most animal behavior issues can be resolved by patiently and consistently teaching basic obedience. If, however, you find that you are experiencing persistent behavior problems with your pet, particularly if those problems threaten the safety of your children or other people, you should consult an animal behaviorist. These specialists require direct contact with you and your animal to render a diagnosis and recommend treatment and do not guarantee results. Usually, a positive outcome will be largely dependent on the owner's diligence in following through with a treatment plan. Animal behaviorists will have completed graduate study in animal behavior or a related field and will be certified (or can demonstrate eligibility for certification) by the Animal Behavior Society, the Association of Companion Animal Behavior Counselors, or the American College of Veterinary Behaviorists.[12] Although more costly than standard obedience training, such expert consultation can pay huge dividends in helping you to avoid a tragic outcome for your pet, members of your family, and others.

TOYS AND OTHER THINGS

Pets, like children, enjoy toys. And, as with children, it is important to select toys that are safe. Some dogs have very "soft" mouths and can be trusted to play with cloth or stuffed dog toys. Others will shred them and may ingest parts that can cause digestive problems. Those dogs are better off with hard rubber or plastic toys that can withstand their vigorous chewing. Toys that may present risk related to entanglement or choking should also be avoided. Cats, for example, may enjoy hanging toys that they can bat, but attaching them to a spring may be safer than suspending them from a cord that can become wrapped around the kitty's neck or swallowed.

Problems often arise when children and pets try to enjoy the *same* toys in very different ways or when animals decide to play with people possessions that are not toys at all. The acquisition of a pet, particularly if it is a dog, may be the time for your children, and perhaps you as well, to have a crash course in keeping personal and household items that the dog might appropriate as a toy out of the dog's reach. One of us was reminded of that lesson recently when her sheltie plucked her leather wallet out of a purse left carelessly open on the floor. The wallet was not so different from his leather chew toys, and it was on the floor where his toys usually are, so he logically assumed it was okay to chew. What was in order was not punishment for the dog but a self-scolding for the owner. Here are a few considerations about the selection and use of pet toys that may help you and your children avoid similar experiences as well as conflict between children and animals where possessions are concerned.

First, when selecting toys for your pet, think about whether the characteristics of the item being considered will allow the animal to easily distinguish between it and other objects that are off-limits. Items such as old shoes and slippers are clearly poor candidates for chew toys. Your puppy may be really smart, but chances are he can't distinguish between a discarded leather slipper and your pricey new shoes. Some other potential problems with candidate toys may be less obvious, however. For example, but for its squeaker, that flat, floppy shaped-like-a-bone cloth dog toy may not feel or taste a lot different from the edge of the Oriental rug in your hallway. And Fido certainly can't be expected to distinguish between a teddy bear dog toy and the precious teddy that your three-year-old cannot spend a night without.

Children will need to be clearly instructed about leaving out objects that may be harmful to or that may be harmed by their pet. And when lapses occur, as they inevitably will, it is not the pet who deserves to be punished. For the child, the loss or damage of the object itself may be sufficient consequence to encourage greater care with possessions in the future.

A family pet is a "family" responsibility and certainly children can participate in caring for a pet. Learning to be responsible is one of the greatest benefits derived from raising children with pets. But caring for a pet is a *big* responsibility, one that children cannot shoulder on their own. Parents need to supervise, coordinate, and play an active role in caring for the pet.

CARING AND LEARNING

But even with their age-related limitations, children can certainly assume a role in pet care. And they can learn a lot from taking care of pets. They learn compassion in caring for a living creature that needs them. They learn time management as they turn off the TV or take a break from a school project to walk or feed the pet. They learn responsibility and the consequences that go along with it when the pet's health depends on them.

For parents, though, it is important to fit the responsibility to the child's ability. Within a span of a few years, especially between the ages of about four and seven, children develop motor skills at somewhat different rates. The dexterity required to complete tasks associated with pet care are the same as those children use for many other activities: trying to help Mom or Dad in the house or yard, playing games with their friends, managing their own food, and so on.

So consider what you have observed about your child in these situations and apply it to your expectations in relation to helping with pet-care chores like walking or feeding the dog or changing the litter pan. Preschoolers can "help" with many pet care tasks when closely supervised by parents or an older sibling. But if your child can't keep his ice cream on the cone or carry his own popcorn at the movie, it's likely he won't have much better luck struggling solo to get a pan of wet litter to the garbage can or carry a full bowl of water.

Managing Change

Few things about parenting are as predictable as the need to deal with change; this goes for changes in family pet care practices as well. From the minute children enter the world, they are changing. Kids change not only as a product of normal development but, as they get older, in response to the multiple demands of their school and social activities. This means that their availability for and interest in pet care will change as well. Anticipating and planning for the impact of this change will help avoid missed meals for Fluffy or walks for Fido and irritation on the part of Mom, Dad, or a sibling when pet care tasks suddenly fall to one of them.

So, when ball practice or rehearsals for the school play will mean that the pet's primary caregiver will be getting home from school two hours later, it is best to decide beforehand how pet care will be handled. You, the parent, will of course need to raise the issue; otherwise, your child will likely just assume that you will handle the task in his absence. But helping to plan for his pet's needs to be met despite his change in schedule is a good life lesson for any youngster even if Mom or Dad *does* finally end up taking up the slack.

Adolescents, in particular, may become less involved with a pet as they move to more independence. Developmentally, teens are *supposed* to become more interested in spending time with their friends and in activities that take them out of the home. This, then, is to be expected and is one reason why it's important that other members of the family also have a commitment to the animal. It is a good idea to directly address the fact that the new responsibilities or interests of the older youth mean less time spent with the pet and make plans as to how the animal's needs, not just for basic care, but for attention and affection, will be met.

Helping Hands

Almost all children beyond the age of toddlers can help with feeding the family pet, they just may not be able to do it all on their own. Allow your child to share in pet care tasks, but set reasonable expectations for the child. You can't expect a third grader to walk down a grocery store aisle and choose the best food for the new kitten. He might choose the brand that has the cutest kitty depicted *on* the bag with little concern for what's *in* the bag. If you don't let your child shop for his own dinner, why let him shop for your pet's dinner?

And you can't expect a young child to monitor the water level in the pet's bowl all by himself either. If something good comes on TV, a neighbor comes over to play, or homework is looming, water duty may be forgotten.

Feeding a pet can afford an opportunity for children's learning in areas other than care-giving and taking responsibility. They learn a little about nutrition while shopping with their parents for pet food. Compare pet food to human food and discuss the fact that both animals and humans need nutritious diets. The difference is that humans have to consume a variety of foods to complete their nutritional requirements, but dogs and cats only have to eat one fully balanced food. This is also a good time to explain that pets don't get bored with their food; thus it is neither necessary nor advisable for children (or adults) to vary the pet's diet by sharing their own food.

Children enjoy "helping" at pet mealtime and if properly taught, they really *can* be a help. Place a small plastic measuring cup in the pet food bag and teach your child how to measure the proper amount per serving. Feeding time can also double as a quick math lesson as the child calculates the food portions. Let's see . . . if the dog should eat one full cup per day and he is fed twice daily, how much food should be given at each meal?

There are consequences associated with failure to live up to any responsibility. If your child fails to do his homework, he may get a lower grade in class. If she fails to clean her room, she may miss the Friday night party. But if your child fails to feed and water the dog or cat, the consequences are even more significant. Children should be taught to understand that the pet's health depends on their ability to provide these essentials, so this task is a responsibility with "mortal consequences." What a great lesson for any child.

"ALL ALONE AM I": NEGLECTED PETS

Animals are not inanimate toys that are there to be picked up and put down at the owner's whim. And their needs are not limited to the times when we are available and thinking about them. While animals want some time to themselves, they also require plenty of interaction with the human members of their family. As is the case with children, more pets probably suffer from neglect than from abuse.[13] And as with children, neglect may be even more harmful to an animal's well-being than overt abuse.

Avoiding neglect is not just about the well-being of the pet, but of your kids as well. If you got your children a pet so that they could derive benefits from that relationship, remember that those benefits come from time spent with the animal, not just from having it in a kennel or out in the backyard.

Some research has shown that humans engage their pets at their own whim; it is typically the human who breaks off interaction with the pet rather the other way around.[14] Especially with today's busy lifestyles, you may need to encourage your children to spend active time with a pet. This is especially true if you have a dog, but cats need consistent attention also.

You may be a parent who favors using a Grandma's Law approach to discipline (as in "If you eat your vegetables, you can have dessert" or "If you make your bed and put your dirty clothes in the laundry basket, you can go outside and ride your bike"). If you are, hats off to you; Grandma's Law has a pretty good track record. It connects behavior to consequences and gives kids some choices in the process. If, however, you are inclined to include the child's pet in the Grandma's Law bargain, be sure that the consequence for noncompliance accrues to the child, not the animal. For example, not being able to have a game of Frisbee with Fido is an acceptable consequence for a child's noncompliance only if Fido will still have plenty of other opportunities for exercise and companionship that day. Withholding or threatening to withhold basic care from a pet is never an appropriate punishment for a child.

"KIDS CAN BE CRUEL": ANIMAL ABUSE

We've all heard it said that kids can be cruel. Usually this statement refers to children's treatment of each other, but it can be true of their treatment of animals as well. It should go without saying that children must not be allowed to abuse pets. You are not likely to encounter intentional severe maltreatment of pets by your children. Children may sometimes inadvertently hurt animals, particularly if they have not been instructed in their proper handling, but they do not do so deliberately under normal circumstances. Tail twisting or rough handling by a toddler during play, though it should be guarded against, is not animal cruelty.

Although legal definitions vary, animal abuse is generally the deliberate infliction of injury or pain on an animal done either in anger or for "fun" or any sexual stimulation of an animal. When such behavior does occur, it is cause for alarm and should never be ignored as just "kids being kids." A substantial body of research links childhood animal cruelty to violent crime as well as to a range of other antisocial behavior.[15] This behavior may be an early indicator of serious trouble ahead for your child. As a parent, you must immediately take steps to stop the behavior, understand and address its cause, and protect the animal from any future occurrences. This situation calls for professional consultation. Your pediatrician may be a good place to start.

As a parent, you can help prevent cruelty as well as inadvertent mistreatment by ensuring that you and the other adults in your child's life set an example of kindness toward humans and animals. It is your responsibility to handle and speak to animals calmly and gently and to communicate to your child that it is wrong to treat animals cruelly.

VENTURING OUT

Children develop their earliest understanding of rules, customs, and relationships within their families and apply that learning to new experiences in the larger world. This holds true with regard to their behavior with both people and animals. Thus, pet-owning children may well assume that all animals, whether of the same or a different species, can be treated in the same way that they treat their pet.

It is important that children receive instruction about interacting with animals who are unknown to them. We tend to recognize the importance of this most often in the case of dogs, knowing that a strange dog may be aggressive. Children should be taught neither to approach nor to run from a strange dog. In addition, teaching them (and having them practice) what is sometimes called the "possum stance" can also help keep children safe when they are approached by a strange dog.[16] This entails standing absolutely still with chin tucked and arms folded across their torso. But children need instruction with regard to other pets as well, so that animal encounters at the homes of friends or wherever else they might be don't go awry.

Wise parents will inquire about the animals present in households that their children will visit. If, for example, you have a dog and your five-year-old daughter is going to visit a friend who has a cat or a rabbit, it might be appropriate to talk with her about how cats and rabbits behave differently from dogs, and particularly how one might interact differently with them than with a dog. Rabbits, for example, don't like to be held, and they may kick or scratch, injuring themselves as well as the child. Cats may also scratch if they are picked up when they don't want to be, may not be allowed to go outside, and so on.

LEARNING ABOUT THE BIRDS AND THE BEES

Many parents wonder whether they should allow their female dog or cat to have at least one litter of young as an educational opportunity for their children. We have only one answer to that question: *NO! Absolutely, unequivocally, and emphatically, no!* And this applies not only to mixed breeds but to purebred animals as well. Many people assume that since their animal is a registered purebred, it should be allowed to reproduce. That assumption is incorrect. Registration provides no guarantee that an animal does not have characteristics that should not be passed on through breeding.

Backyard breeding is also not a great way to bring in extra money. Responsible breeders are more interested in improving their breed than in earning money, and many spend more than they earn in the enterprise. They invest considerable effort and expense in learning about their breed's characteristics and bloodlines, and in planning a breeding program that is designed to produce healthy animals with desirable physical and temperament traits. They examine pedigrees; test breeding animals for disease and inheritable defects;

socialize their animals' offspring; prepare sale contracts that include protections for the buyer, breeder, and (especially) for the animal itself; and screen prospective buyers. If you are not willing to do *all* of these things, please neuter your animal, whether male or female, as soon as your veterinarian determines that it is medically safe to do so. Earlier neutering can also be beneficial by preventing hormone-related problems such as mammary (breast) tumors and prostatic hyperplasia (enlarged prostate), discouraging roaming, and improving behavior.

Recognize, too, that amateur breeders face a real risk of winding up with something other than the purebred litter for which they hoped. If you think you can detect your female animal's approaching estrus ("season") more accurately than any of the fertile male animals in your neighborhood, think again. Unless you are prepared to maintain full control over access to your fertile female cat or dog at all times, "accidents" not only can, but almost certainly *will* happen.

Don't set a bad example for your children by breeding animals that will contribute to the severe pet overpopulation problem we already have in the United States. There are better ways to teach your children about reproduction and to earn a few extra dollars.

CHAPTER SUMMARY

Points to Remember

- All children who are old enough to understand should be instructed in the treatment and handling of animals.
- Infants and toddlers should never be left alone with an animal.
- Ensuring children's safety with pets is as much about teaching them how to interact with the animal as it is about managing animal behavior.
- Pets need a place for some protected quiet time away from children.
- Children can help with feeding and watering the pet, but these are important responsibilities and should be supervised by an adult.
- Safety issues may arise with dogs when the dog views a child as an equal or inferior in the family "pack."

- Companion animals serve important functions as confidants and playmates for children and may be viewed by young children much as siblings are.
- Neglect is a danger for many companion animals given today's busy lifestyles.
- Deliberately abusive behavior toward animals is not normal childhood behavior and warrants immediate action by parents to stop the behavior and secure professional help for their child.
- Children should not assume that it is safe to interact with strange animals (even those belonging to friends) in the same way they do with their own pets.
- Animals (even registered purebreds) should not be bred to provide sex education for children or to boost the family income.

Child-Pet Interaction Checklist

√ Develop a household policy that ensures that infants and very young children will never be left alone with a pet. Last one out of a room grabs either the baby or the pet.

√ Instruct your children to allow some downtime for the pet and establish a quiet place where the animal can have some refuge.

√ Include the pet as much as possible in family activities.

√ Encourage your children to include their pets in quiet activities such as reading and watching television as well as in play.

√ Instruct your children about interaction with animals other than their own (strange dogs and cats as well as those of their friends).

√ If you notice behavior that is deliberately abusive to an animal, take action immediately. If it is with your own child, seek professional help; if it is a friend of your child, contact his or her parents. They need to know.

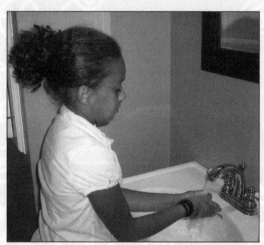

Photo by Gwen Rutkowski

CHAPTER 6

THE YUCKY SIDE OF PETS
Addressing the Potential Health Risks
Pets Pose to Children

Pets give us so many nice things: wet kisses, warm hugs, lots of laughs. Unfortunately, they have the potential to give us a few things that aren't so nice.

Even the sweetest pets can infect people with diseases. Any such illness that is transmitted from animals to people is called a *zoonotic* disease. Zoonotic diseases include bacterial, fungal, viral, and parasitic infections. Besides being carriers of illnesses, dogs and cats are also implicated in human allergies. The role pets play in human allergies has not been categorically defined as good or bad, but their names always come up on the suspect list.

IT'S A ZOO OUT THERE: SIMPLIFYING ZOONOSES

Zoonotic diseases can be complicated ailments. The purpose of this chapter is to simplify the subject of common zoonotic diseases, because (as with many scary subjects) the more you understand, the less fearful you will be.

The fear of zoonoses should not keep you from getting a pet nor should it make you relinquish one you already have. With commonsense precautions, you can protect your family from zoonotic diseases. But first, you have to know what the enemy does, where it lives, and what it looks like.

PARASITES: UNWELCOME VISITORS

Ever have a visitor who comes into your home uninvited and then overstays his welcome? You begin to feel like you're hosting a parasite, right? Well, think of intestinal worms as a large parasitic family that comes uninvited into your home (i.e., your body or your pet's body) and refuses to leave until you force them to do so. Let's look at some of the parasites eager to move in.

ROUNDWORMS REALLY DO GET AROUND

One of the most imposing zoonotic parasites is the roundworm (*Toxocara canis, Toxocara cati*). The roundworm is aptly named because the eggs are round. Adult worms are long and stringy, kind of like spaghetti.

The roundworm can enter the pet's body in several ways, depending on the age of the pet. Puppies and kittens can acquire an immature stage of the parasite while in the womb or can become infected after birth while nursing. Transmammary infection (via nursing) is more common in dogs than in cats.

Dogs and cats of any age can also become infected by ingesting worm eggs directly from their environment. Eggs shed in the feces of infected dogs and cats infest the soil and can be picked up by other dogs and cats.

Regardless of the mode of transmission (in utero, by nursing, or by ingestion), these roundworm eggs go through a complicated migratory pattern in the pet's body, develop during their migration, and end up in the intestinal tract as adults.

After becoming adjusted to their new intestinal tract home, adult female worms start a family of their own and produce offspring in the form of eggs. The eggs quickly leave home and enter the big outside world so they can find their own homes. The eggs exit the pet's GI (gastrointestinal) tract in the stool and inhabit the soil where they are deposited. In the soil, the eggs undergo developmental changes while they search for a new home (i.e., a new pet to infect).

Roundworm eggs are patient. They take their time in finding a new home. They are well protected by a sturdy shell that can withstand extremes in climate. They will survive hot, dry summers and cold, wet winters while waiting for the best opportunity to infect an appropriate host.

The house-hunting eggs enter their new home through a wide open door (i.e., the pet's mouth). Dogs and cats become infected by eating soil, licking grass, or licking themselves after they lie on the grass. Transmission of a parasite from the stool to the mouth in this manner is called "fecal-oral transmission."

Once in the pet, the eggs develop, move around, and eventually become adults. As adults, they do what their ancestors did: They reproduce more eggs to continue the life cycle.

Human Roundworm Infection

The zoonotic problem arises because these parasites will enter any open door . . . a cat mouth, a dog mouth, a human mouth. They'll invade any mouth and be quite happy with the new home that awaits them. And we, as humans, provide them with ample open doors.

Picture this scene: Your son plays in the mud, or picks up his baseball after it rolls on the grass, or digs in the sand box, then runs indoors and grabs a chocolate chip cookie without washing his hands. There you have it: fecal-oral transmission.

Any time a person contacts anything contaminated with dog or cat stool and then touches something that goes in the mouth, transmission of a zoonotic parasite like the roundworm is possible. See how easy it is for us to leave the door open for roundworms?

The New Human Neighborhood

Once inside the mouth, the roundworms enter the human GI tract. But these unwelcome visitors aren't always pleased with their intestinal home. They prefer to look around a bit before settling down. The swallowed eggs hatch in the GI tract and release larvae that are the actual roundworm house-hunters. The larval house-hunting trip is called migration.

The roundworm larvae may travel through many other areas of the body before they pick a permanent home. The location of this new roundworm home determines the type of illness they cause in their host. If the worm decides to live in the liver, the person might develop liver disease; if the worm sets up housekeeping in the lungs, the person may have respiratory complications; if the worm lives in the eye, the person may have vision deficits; if the worm takes a trip all the way to the brain, the person could exhibit neurologic symptoms.

Since human illness is caused during the migration of the larvae, the resulting human disease caused by these roaming parasites is known as *larval migrans*. If the migration ends up in a major organ such as the liver or lungs, the disease is called *visceral* larval migrans. If the migration ends up in the eye, the illness is referred to as *ocular* larval migrans. If in the brain, it is called *neural* larval migrans. All larval house-hunting expeditions could mean trouble for the human host whose body is being invaded by the unwelcome guests.

Roundworms do not complete their life cycle in humans. Our bodies do not provide the proper environment for larvae to develop into egg-producing adults. So humans with roundworm infection do not infect other humans or animals. However, the presence of this parasite can be quite devastating.

Incidence of Roundworm Infection in Humans

Roundworm infection sounds scary, and it is. Obviously, roundworms are not tenants we humans want around. How often does human infection occur? How many of us are playing unsuspecting landlords to these parasites? Do parents need to be concerned about roundworm infection?

It's difficult to arrive at a definite number of roundworm-infected people. Some people don't even know they are infected because they aren't sick at all or are only mildly ill. Their larvae may have landed in an area of the body and remained quiet tenants. So these infected people are not counted in the census.

Those people who do become sick are sometimes misdiagnosed. But even those who see a doctor and are diagnosed with roundworm infection are not always counted as the victim of a zoonotic disease because doctors do not always report the infection to the Centers for Disease Control (CDC).

Due to unrecognized, undiagnosed, and unreported human roundworm infections, the incidence of this zoonotic disease is difficult to ascertain; therefore, the CDC statistics are probably lower than the actual infection rate. But even considering this, the CDC receives three thousand to four thousand serum samples a year from patients with a presumptive diagnosis of roundworm infection.[1] In a sample of more than twenty thousand people, 13.9 percent had a positive titer to *Toxocara*, indicating previous exposure. The exposure rate was higher in males (15.9 percent) than in females (12.4 percent). These are sobering figures.[2]

To further illustrate the significance of roundworm infection, the ocular disease caused by parasite migration is startling. It is estimated that approximately ten thousand people in the United States suffer from roundworm invasion of the eye every year. People with ocular larval migrans develop inflammatory eye disease, and many of them suffer partial or total vision loss. In fact, 95 percent of ocular larval migrans patients develop faulty vision, and 20 percent become blind in one or both eyes.[3]

So, should parents be concerned about roundworm infection in their children? They should certainly be aware of the infection potential, but should also realize how easy it is to reduce or eliminate exposure to roundworms. With proper precautions, there should be no cause for concern.

HOOKWORMS: ANOTHER UNWELCOME VISITOR

Another zoonotic parasite is the hookworm. Hookworm transmission is a little different from that of roundworms in two ways. Like roundworms, hookworms infect dogs and cats as they are nursing, but unlike roundworms, hookworms rarely infect pups and kittens in the uterus.

Second, hookworms have another mode of infection. The hookworm is sometimes an impatient door knocker. Rather than wait around for an open door (mouth) to its new home, the hookworm often sneaks into the house through a back way.

In the larval stage, hookworms can invade the animal or human body directly through the skin. Usually this occurs through the bottoms of the feet, which can have frequent contact with the ground where the hookworm larvae are. Dogs obviously have lots of foot-to-ground contact, but people who run barefoot in the yard or play on sandy beaches may be exposed to hookworm larvae as well.

Once infected, dogs and cats provide a good home for the larvae to mature; the hosts then harbor adult hookworms in their intestinal tracts. These adults lay eggs that are eliminated in the stool and contaminate the environment while waiting on the next host.

Hookworms that find an open door through the mouth enter the intestinal tract and can cause GI disturbances after they set up residence there. People with intestinal hookworm infections may have intestinal problems similar to irritable bowel syndrome.

Hookworms that enter the host through the skin cause dermatological disorders. Once in the skin, hookworm larval migration can be easily followed because larvae leave behind obvious tracks—red lines that delineate the migratory path of hookworms. The human skin lesions are usually not severe and are unlikely to leave any permanent scarring.

Hairy dogs and cats usually do not show evidence of dermal hookworm migration, but people readily reveal evidence of infection. In fact, a veterinarian's daughter was infected with hookworms after a visit to the beach and bore distinct evidence of the infection as red migrating tract lines on her feet and buttocks. Zoonotic hookworm infection can affect anyone even people without pets.

Since hookworm migrations are usually superficial or confined to the intestinal tract, the effects of hookworm zoonosis is not as devastating as roundworm migrations. Hookworms are not usually associated with major liver, lung, or central nervous system disease but can be a significant heath issue for pets and people nonetheless.

HANDLING UNWANTED GUESTS: HOW TO PREVENT OR EVICT PARASITES

The exact number of human cases of zoonotic infection by hookworms and roundworms eludes us. Larval migrans syndromes are not reportable in the United States, so the actual number of human cases is unknown. However, many human cases continue to be diagnosed and a recent national survey of shelters revealed that almost 36 percent of dogs nationwide harbored helminthes (worms) capable of causing human disease.[4]

If almost 40 percent of dogs have parasites that can harm people, it makes sense to have a game plan to deal with them. Our first line of defense is to clean up the infection at the source, that is, the dog and cat. So, let's evict these unwanted guests from our pets.

There are many effective medications to treat existing infections and many more to prevent future infections of hookworms and roundworms in our pets. By eliminating the parasites in our pets, we not only improve their health, we significantly reduce human exposure to these worms. All pet owners, but especially those with children, need to be diligent about giving their dogs and cats year-round monthly parasite control medications upon the advice of their veterinarian.

Zoonotic parasites sound scary, but they don't have to be. We can simply deny residence to roundworms and hookworms by taking a few simple precautions.

1. Clean up after your pet eliminates in the yard. Picking up stool deposits will reduce seeding of the yard with infective eggs. This isn't a fun job, but it is necessary.

2. Make sure that children (and adults) wash their hands thoroughly after spending time outdoors and after contacting the pet directly.
3. Do not go outdoors on the grass or on the beach barefoot.
4. Visit your veterinarian at least twice annually and have fecal exams performed. Place dogs and cats on year-round parasite control medication. Eliminating infection in pets greatly reduces human exposure to these parasites.

In an effort to standardize parasite prevention protocols in veterinary practices, a national committee of veterinarians, parasitologists, and human health professionals was formed. This group, the Companion Animal Parasite Council (CAPC), recognizes that keeping pets parasite free contributes to their health and the health of their human families. CAPC recommends placing all dogs and cats on year-round, monthly, broad spectrum parasite medication. Talk to your veterinarian about which medication is best for your pet and your family. Two very good Web sites for further information about parasites are www.petsandparasites.org and www.growingupwithpets.com.

The bottom line is this: Children who wash their hands and keep their shoes on should not be at risk for roundworm or hookworm infection. So let's enjoy our pets and our children while our children enjoy our pets.

HEARTWORMS: THE PARASITE WITHOUT A HEART

Monthly parasite prevention not only helps with intestinal parasites like hookworms and roundworms but can also prevent heartworms. Adult heartworms live in the heart and in the pulmonary artery. Heartworms are transmitted to dogs and cats through a mosquito bite. Although this parasite is rarely zoonotic, it is important to understand how heartworms affect our pets and us.

Mosquitoes harbor an immature form of the heartworm, called a larva, within their bodies. When an infected mosquito bites a dog, it deposits larvae as it sucks blood out of the dog. The larva migrates through the dog's body and eventually sets up housekeeping in the pet's pulmonary artery. Here the larvae grow into adult heartworms that look a little like the intestinal roundworm. In other words, here's another parasite that looks like pasta.

Once they are settled in their new home, adult heartworms reproduce more babies (larvae) that begin circulating through the dog's bloodstream waiting for the next mosquito to come along and give them a ride to their new home. When the next mosquito bites the infected dog, it acquires these new larvae, which develop inside the mosquito's body before being injected into the next dog or cat unlucky enough to get bitten. It is important to note that dogs cannot give heartworms directly to each other, to a cat, or to a person. The intermediary mosquito is necessary to transmit this parasite.

Mosquitoes, Heartworms, and People

Sometimes a heartworm-carrying mosquito bites a human and injects the larvae into a person instead of a dog. Luckily, heartworm infection in people is not the cardiopulmonary disease that plagues dogs and cats. Even so, a bite from a heartworm-carrying mosquito can lead to human illness.

After the mosquito injects a larva into a person, the larva migrates through the person's body and eventually sets up residence. Heartworm larvae may live underneath the skin or in deeper locations such as major organs.

The heartworm larva prefers a private neighborhood so the human body builds a fence around larva by surrounding it in fibrous tissue. The fibrous tissue that forms the larva's fence is called a granuloma. In the center of the granuloma is the actual heartworm larva.

Granulomas may be superficial on extremities that are exposed to mosquito bites like arms and legs or may be in deeper organs like lung or liver tissue. While these lesions are not usually serious, they often cause enough problems that they need to be surgically removed.

Human Heartworm Transmission

It's important to understand that just because you have a dog or cat, you aren't any more likely to get heartworm disease than is your neighbor who doesn't own a pet at all. Since mosquitoes travel, they may bite a dog in one neighborhood and acquire a heartworm larva, then bite a person down the block infecting him. So, unlike other zoonotic diseases, *your* dog may not be the culprit in human heartworm infection.

Human Heartworm Prevention

CAPC recommends that all cats and dogs be given a monthly heartworm preventive year-round. This is especially important in warmer climates where mosquito populations prevail. Reducing the number of infective larvae in our pets may reduce the number of larvae around to infect us.

It's also a good idea for people to wear long sleeve shirts and pants when outside at dusk. Mosquito repellants are also helpful when spending time outside in mosquito-infested areas.

To decrease mosquito infestation in your yard, remove all sources of standing water such as children's play pools and empty planters. Fill in any holes that Rover may have dug so that they don't retain water.

With a little yard work, consistent heartworm medications for our pets, and the usual mosquito avoidance tactics, heartworm infection should not be a worry for people.

RINGWORM: NOT A WORM AT ALL

Despite its name, ringworm is a fungus, not a worm. This fungal infection gets its name from the characteristic ring-shaped skin lesion it causes in humans.

Humans become infected with ringworm through close contact with an infected dog or cat or from a contaminated environment. How do you know that your pet is infected? Don't look for rings. Pet lesions do not take the shape of a ring, but appear as crusty areas of hair loss usually on the face, feet, or ears.

Young pups and kittens with immature immune systems are more commonly infected than are adult pets; however, humans of all ages are susceptible, especially those who are immunosuppressed.

People tend to get these ring-shaped lesions on the exposed areas of the body that come into direct contact with the pet. If you picture a young child hugging his new kitten or puppy, you'll understand why most human lesions occur on the forearms and neck.

Human infections can be effectively treated with topical medications, but if the pet's infection is not cleared sufficiently, reinfection can occur. Veterinarians often utilize oral as well as topical medications in treating this fungal infection in dogs and cats.

Since concurrent treatment of both two-legged and four-legged family members provides the best response, it's imperative for human lesions to be evaluated by a physician while pet lesions are evaluated by a veterinarian.

CAT FIGHT! RETRACT THOSE CLAWS OR ELSE

One zoonotic disease blamed entirely on felines is cat-scratch fever. Here, the name says it all. Humans may develop fever, as well as lethargy and enlarged lymph nodes, following a cat scratch.

Cat-scratch fever is caused by a bacterium called *Bartonella henselae*. Here's how *Bartonella* gets around. A cat that carries *B. henselae* has been bitten by a flea that sucks the cat's blood. Then the flea defecates on the cat and deposits feces that contain the bacteria. Next, the cat scratches itself and collects the bacteria under its' claws. Finally, when the cat scratches a human, it contaminates the wound with the bacteria. Sometimes, humans are infected from direct exposure to flea feces, without receiving a cat scratch.

Infected humans may have a fever, malaise, and swollen lymph nodes. Since many cat-inflicted wounds occur on the forearms, the axillary (under the arm) lymph nodes are most often enlarged.

Quick, thorough cleansing of a cat scratch will decrease the potential to develop a bacterial infection. Medical care should be promptly sought if symptoms arise. Human infections are treated with antibiotics but can be prevented altogether by taking a couple of precautions.

First, keep your cat flea free by using one of the monthly flea-control medications. Second, keep cat nails trimmed, or use nail caps on your cat (Soft Paws). These can be quickly applied in the veterinary hospital or even at home. Some cat owners choose to declaw the cat (a somewhat controversial procedure), which reduces the incidence of cat-scratch fever and furniture demolition at the same time. This is a serious surgery that should be discussed with your veterinarian.

THAT MANGY MUTT: CANINE AND HUMAN SARCOPTES INFECTION

OK, now to even the score, let's talk about a zoonotic infection predominately attributed to exposure to dogs: sarcoptic mange, or scabies. Sarcoptic mange is caused by a very small mite that makes its home deep in the canine hair follicle. This mite causes extreme pruritus (itching) in the dog and hair loss mostly on the ears, elbows, and legs.

People can pick up the mite from their dogs, but the mite is also found in the environment, so people can become infected even without direct contact with a dog. Many cases, however, can be attributed to canine contact.

Scabies in people results in a series of small, reddened "bite" lesions that occur on areas of contact such as forearms and necks. Lesions also have a tendency to accumulate in areas under the waistband of pants and under socks on the ankle.

Immunosuppressed people are most at risk for scabies; luckily the skin condition is readily treated with topical medications. And, what a relief. People don't lose their hair to sarcoptic mange infection.

ACHOO! PET ALLERGIES

While the relationship between pet ownership and human allergies is still being investigated, currently recognized information regarding people, pets, and allergies is discussed below.

For years, parents of children with a family history of allergies and asthma have avoided pet ownership altogether. When balancing the benefits of having a child grow up with a pet against the risk of having a sick child, pets lost out.

The association of pets to human allergic respiratory disease is under debate and validated studies are hard to find. In the real world, it is difficult to conduct a scientific study that doesn't have loopholes.

For example, while evaluating the allergy risk of pets, people are simultaneously exposed to many other allergens such as dust mites, pollens, and so on. So how are we to know what's really to blame for allergy symptoms—the dog or the dogwood tree?

To evaluate just pet allergies, study subjects would have to live in a "bubble" with only their dog or cat for company. Since that isn't likely to happen, let's keep the study loopholes in mind as we review a few research findings. You may be surprised by what you'll find out.

Allergy Studies: Good News and Bad

In one Swedish study, people were surveyed regarding the incidence of asthma in their families. First and second grade children were followed for three years to assess their incidence of allergy development. It was noted that cat ownership had a significant protective effect against developing asthma, and dog ownership had a similar protective effect, though not as significant. In other words, the kids raised with pets were actually *less likely* to have allergies.[5]

Another study found that exposure of children to pets may increase the indoor endotoxin exposure. That means that a little dirt in the house may actually be good. Early exposure of children to these endotoxins may decrease the development of atopic dermatitis and asthma. The study concluded that allowing cats in a child's bedroom within the first year may actually prevent the development of childhood asthma. Interestingly, children over one year of age who were exposed to cats did not receive the same benefit. So early exposure to cats was more beneficial.[6]

In yet another study, early exposure to cats resulted in an increased risk of developing cat allergies but a decreased risk of developing allergies to airborne allergens, and there was no significant influence on the risk of developing asthma. The same study produced different canine results. Children exposed to dogs early in life did not develop more dog allergies and, furthermore, had a reduced risk of sensitization to airborne allergens and asthma. So this particular study went to the dogs.[7]

Another study surmised that while having animals in the home during a child's early years may be beneficial, this benefit must be weighed against the risk of maintaining a pet in the home with a child or adult who has definite pet allergies. In other words, for parents with asthma who are afraid that their children may have inherited the tendency to develop asthma, acquiring a pet as a protective mechanism is not recommended. Since parents and other siblings may be allergic to the pet, more harm than good may be done in the home. Helping one child may put other family members at risk.

On the other hand, the presence of animals was associated with less sensitization to dogs, cats, and other environmental allergens. Bringing a pet into the home may not be completely protective, but a nonallergic child raised with pets may be less likely to develop allergies later in life.[8]

Before parents get too excited about the prospect that they may decrease a child's allergies by raising them with pets in the home, they must consider the loopholes in research. It may be that the observed linkage between living with pets and a decrease in allergic symptoms and asthma can be explained by the simple fact of selection bias in the families surveyed.

Parents who know they have a family tendency for pet allergies may simply avoid exposure to pets and never acquire one. Similarly, those families that have the pets may be those that know they can tolerate them. In other words, allergic families avoid pets while families that experience a healthy pet-keeping effect are those that can tolerate them anyway. This selection bias may certainly skew any results gathered from family surveys and must be kept in mind.[9]

So, the jury is still out when it comes to pets, people, and allergies. While the debate continues, we can enjoy our pets without relying on the positive allergic associations and hopefully not suffering too much from the negative ones.

TICK-TOCK: TICK TIME BOMBS

Tick-borne illnesses are another class of zoonotic diseases to consider. These illnesses are not contracted directly from the pet but rather from ticks that the pet carries into the yard or home. So, like mosquitoes, ticks are the carriers of the problem but the source of the infection may be the dog.

It's important to realize that people may pick up ticks directly from the environment, so people without pets may also acquire tick-borne illnesses. As with heartworms, we can't blame all tick-borne illnesses on our dogs.

The best known, if not the most common, tick-borne illness is Lyme disease. Lyme disease is named for the area where it was first diagnosed, Old Lyme, Connecticut. The disease is caused by a bacterium called *Borrelia burgdorferi.*

People are infected when they are bitten by a tick that sucks their blood and leaves behind the bacteria. Infected people may develop a rash that spreads from the location of the tick bite. Some people also have flulike symptoms. Sometimes, infected people develop more serious diseases, including meningitis. Fortunately for people and dogs, this scary-sounding disease is usually responsive to antibiotic treatment if caught early.

The best way to avoid Lyme disease or the many other diseases transmitted by ticks is to avoid ticks. Wear long sleeves and pants when in wooded areas. Use insect repellent. Thoroughly check the entire body, including the scalp, for attached ticks.

Ticks are frightening enough even without carrying a disease, so let's avoid them altogether. Keeping your dog tick free may help keep your home and yard tick free. Talk to your veterinarian about the best tick-prevention measure. Also remember that while cats may remove ticks through grooming, they can bring them into the home.

THE GRANDDADDY OF ZOONOSES: RABIES

Probably the oldest and best known zoonotic disease is rabies. Can you conjure up the image of the rabid dog foaming at the mouth? Well, erase that mental picture. Rabies doesn't always appear that way.

Rabies is caused by a virus that enters the human body most often through a bite wound. In the United States, the leading transmitters of rabies to humans aren't dogs or cats at all. Bats are responsible for fifteen out of twenty-three cases, 65 percent, of human rabies infection.[10]

It shouldn't be too hard to avoid getting bitten by a bat, but other wild mammals carry the virus, too. Skunks and raccoons have been associated with human infections. Wildlife are formidable rabies carriers because it is difficult to protect wildlife from the disease although some projects aim to do just that.

Since people, in general, are more apt to be exposed to domestic animals than wild ones, let's focus on rabies in our pets. Responsible pet owners can help prevent rabies by vaccinating their dogs and cats according to local and state guidelines. Vaccinated pets limit our exposure to rabies. Recognizing this fact has prompted most areas to enforce rabies ordinances requiring immunization and registration of pets.

A likely transmission of this zoonotic virus occurs like this. Fido goes for a walk in the woods and meets up with a wild animal. Fido gets bitten by the infected wildlife, develops rabies, then literally bites the hand that feeds him, infecting his owner.

Vaccinating household pets provides an important buffer zone between wildlife and humans. If our dogs and cats are vaccinated, they should not become infected with rabies even if they are bitten by a rabid animal, and in turn, they cannot transmit the infection to us.

Dogs and cats with rabies don't always show signs of the disease, so don't depend on a change of attitude or foaming at the mouth–type symptoms to give you a clue that something is amiss. Prevent rabies by vaccinating your pets and by avoiding bites from dogs, cats, or wildlife. Remember those statistics on the incidence of dog bites. Take obedience training seriously.

A ZOONOTIC NEWCOMER: MRSA

MRSA refers to a strain of the bacteria in the Staphylococcus family that is resistant to many antibiotics, including methicillin. Staphylococcus is not a new bacteria, but the resistant mutation of the bacteria has created a new medical dilemma.

Infection occurs through direct contact with the bacteria and commonly takes the form of superficial skin sores. It can also result in a systemic infection that can affect the respiratory system with severe consequences. Since people and pets can carry staph infections, they can pass the infection back and forth.

It is important to note that most staph infections are not antibiotic resistant and respond readily to treatment; however, MRSA is much more difficult to deal with and usually requires treatment with vancomycin. This treatment is often rendered in the hospital through IV therapy.

Parents need to remember two things before getting too upset over MRSA. First, human infection from pets is not very common. Second, normal hygiene greatly reduces the potential for infection. As usual, stringent precautions need to be taken with immunocompromised individuals.

JUST HOW RISKY *IS* GETTING A PET?

Now that you've learned about some of the dangers pets can potentially expose you to, you may be wondering whether pet ownership is worth the risk. The truth is that with some simple, commonsense precautions, you can ensure that the risk to you and your children is minimal.

The benefits of pet ownership are universally recognized as are the possible infections that can occur. For this reason the American Medical Association adopted a one-health policy in 2007 to encourage communication between health care professionals working with animals and humans. The Companion Animal Parasite Council initiated a veterinary–human health care medical board several years ago focusing on zoonotic diseases. Cooperative efforts such as these can only render positive results for people and pets.

With this in mind, remember that healthy and well-behaved pets are not harmful. Kind and cautious children are in little danger from loving pets. Parents who are well prepared and diligent need not be afraid. And raising children with pets will be a great payback for the effort.

CHAPTER SUMMARY

Points to Remember

- Zoonotic diseases come in many forms—parasitic, fungal, bacterial, and viral. Most can be prevented with a few commonsense precautions.
- Dogs and cats can be kept free of internal and external parasites by administering year-round monthly medications prescribed by your veterinarian according to CAPC (Companion Animal Parasite Council) guidelines.
- Good hygiene practices such as limiting the area where pets eliminate, regularly removing feces from your yard, and frequently cleaning litter boxes help prevent transmission of parasites. Hand-washing is a must.
- Adhering to scheduled vaccinations for your pets helps prevent viral diseases, such as rabies, while good skin care will help decrease exposure to fungal infections, such as ringworm.
- Keeping cats flea free will help protect humans from cat-scratch fever.

Potential Health Risks Checklist

√ Instruct children to thoroughly wash their hands after playing with the pet or playing outside. Let them know that they should never eat without first washing their hands.

√ Clean up fecal deposits in the yard and change litter boxes frequently.

√ Keep feline claws trimmed or consider using nail caps to prevent injury from scratches.

√ Teach children to behave properly around all pets to reduce the risk of bites and scratches (see chapter 5).

√ Report any skin lesions on your dog or cat to the veterinarian. Check children for skin lesions as well and report these to your physician.

√ Make a note on your calendar to schedule your pet's next veterinary checkup and vaccinations.

√ Instruct children to avoid contact with wildlife.

√ Give your pet monthly medications for heartworms, intestinal parasites, and flea and tick control.

Photo by Anne Guedry

References

These Web sites provide additional information about parasites and pets:

www.growingupwithpets.com: "Growing Up with Pets: A Parent's Resource for Raising Happy Kids with Healthy Pets."

www.capcvet.org: "The mission of CAPC [Companion Animal Parasite Council] is to foster animal and human health, while preserving the human-animal bond."

Photo by Linell Champagne

CHAPTER 7

GONE TOO SOON

Helping Children Cope with Pet Loss

While we wish that our beloved pets could be with us forever, that is simply not the case. Eventually we lose them. Companion animals can be lost through various means. They may die, be stolen, wander away, or be relinquished. This chapter is devoted largely to the issue of pet death, but addresses all of the forms of loss.

THE DEATH OF A PET

Almost all our companion animals have substantially shorter life expectancies than we. This means that losing them is part of having them—although definitely not the best part. In modern industrialized societies with advanced medical care, people are living longer. This means that pets are often the first and perhaps the only attachment that children are likely to lose while still in childhood.[1]

When a beloved pet dies, the whole family is sad. Parents, being parents, however, often want to minimize the pain of loss for the children. This is a perfectly understandable response, but not necessarily a healthy one. Sometimes, what is intended to protect can actually do more harm than good.

If you have followed the recommendations in this book concerning the selection of a pet and the nurturing of the child-animal relationship in your family, your children have likely formed a deep bond with their pet. There is ample research evidence that children beyond four or five years of age think of pets as family members and their parents often do as well. Children may confide in pets and spend considerable time interacting with them. The death of such an animal is a significant life event, and the feelings of loss and grief that it engenders are deserving of respect. To dismiss the significance of that loss is to trivialize what your children have experienced as important.[2]

Open Communication

As is generally true in all of life, honesty is the best policy when handling animal loss with children. How you communicate the facts of the animal's death to a child, however, depends largely upon the child's age. Very young and preschool-age children will not comprehend the meaning of death. Infants and young toddlers may not consciously miss the animal although they will sense and react to the distress of other family members. Grade school children begin to understand the meaning of death, and preteens and adolescents fully recognize its finality. These older children will experience grief of varying levels of intensity depending upon their degree of interaction with and emotional attachment to the pet.

Children's questions and comments in response to being told of the death of a pet will provide cues to their level of understanding. Parents should answer these questions as honestly and simply as possible. For example, the answer when a child asks whether Fluffy is coming back is something like "No, animals do not come back to us when they die." Your religious beliefs may dictate your response to any questions children ask about where the pet goes after death, but here again, you should be gentle but honest. If you really believe that our pets go to heaven (and many people do), then say so, but do not assure your child of it if you believe otherwise. He will later recognize what your true beliefs are and know that you lied to him.

The reactions of children will also be affected by the circumstances of an animal's death. Any time a pet dies, children should be told what happened simply and directly insofar as you know. Occasionally, an animal will die unexpectedly from a natural but unknown cause. More often, however, the pet will have become old or ill or been injured, and you will thus have more information about the cause of the animal's death.

Acknowledging the cause of death brings closure more readily for the child and the parent; however, if the circumstances surrounding the pet's demise are more than the child can handle, the conversation can be tempered. For example, following the gruesome death of a dog who sustained thoracic trauma from a car accident, a child may be told simply that the dog was so badly injured that the doctor could not make him well again. The child does not need a physiology lesson or a detailed postmortem. If you want your veterinarian to speak with your child, you should talk to the doctor first so she can adjust her medical explanation to your child's level of understanding.

Grief is a normal human response to loss and there will be little you can or should do to prevent your children's experiencing it when a beloved animal dies. Guilt, however, is another matter. If parents recognize the potential for children to feel guilt related to the animal's death they may be able to prevent or minimize it. Guilt may arise from several factors. Younger children may experience "magical thinking" in which they believe that they can actually cause events to occur by wishing for them. So, if your six-year-old happened to become really angry at Fluffy for something and wished for her to go away shortly before the animal died, your child may believe that her wish was fulfilled through the pet's death.

A pet may also die under some circumstance that causes a child to think she was negligent or to feel bad that there was not an opportunity for her to say good-bye. In still other situations, the animal's death may have been related to an action or inaction on the part of a child or the child may perceive that it was. If, for example, the child accidentally left the gate open and Fido went out and was hit by a car, she may well blame herself for the animal's death.

If your family loses a pet under circumstances in which you suspect your child might feel guilty, do not be afraid to discuss this with the child in a direct way. Children must learn that we all make mistakes; sometimes our mistakes have serious consequences that we cannot reverse. Learning from mistakes is constructive; blaming ourselves for them is not.

Anticipated Death

When an animal's death appears imminent, share this news with your children and ask them whether they wish to spend some special time with the pet to say good-bye. Children may want to bring the animal a favorite toy, a blanket, or some other item that they feel will convey a sense of comfort or simply to visit with the pet.

If you and your veterinarian have decided that euthanasia is the most humane option for your pet and you have time, share this news with your children. Explain to them what will happen and why it is necessary to end the animal's life in this way. An older child may ask to be present when the animal dies. That is a decision that you and your child should make together, perhaps in consultation with your veterinarian. It is important, however, that you and the child both fully understand the procedure before the decision is made. Your pet's doctor can explain the process of euthanasia to you. If your children are younger or you decide that they should not be present during the process, your being there will allow you to reassure them that you were able to comfort the animal.

Remember that, as difficult as the loss of a pet is, it provides parents with an opportunity to demonstrate both compassion and courage. Relinquishing a dying pet to a veterinary clinic or animal shelter and turning your back in an attempt to avoid the pain associated with the animal's death demonstrates to children that painful circumstances in life are best avoided rather than dealt with. An animal that has shared your life and provided you and your children with companionship deserves more than that, and your children deserve to learn a better lesson from you.

Healing Rituals

Just as in human death, rituals have their place in the commemoration and mourning of animals. Children as well as adults can gain comfort from pet funerals or family gatherings centered on memories of a cherished animal. Children may be helped by looking at pictures of the pet, sharing their best memories of time spent with Fido or Fluffy, selecting toys to be buried with the pet, or placing flowers on a grave. If your pet is cremated, you may choose to place its ashes along with a picture in a special place in the house or to scatter the ashes in a shady spot in the yard or outside of a favorite window. One young child we know placed a handmade marker at the backyard grave of her hamster. Skittles's grave site was sufficiently meaningful to her that she returned for visits even after her family had moved away.

Children need time to grieve and parents may need to give them permission to take that time and see that others do also. Teachers, child care providers, and perhaps others with whom children are closely associated outside of the family should be informed when a child loses a pet so that they will understand if the child behaves differently for a while.

LOSING A PET THROUGH THEFT OR DISAPPEARANCE

Even if you have followed our recommendations to prevent your pet's wandering off or being stolen (see chapter 4), this can sometimes occur. If anything, losing a pet due to theft or disappearance can be even harder for both you and your children because you are wondering where the animal is, whether it is hurt, how it is being treated, and whether it will ever return.

Children who are school age to teens will usually feel better when they are able to participate in efforts to find their lost pet. If, for example, you judge that your neighborhood is sufficiently safe, children may be encouraged to participate in canvassing the neighbors to see if they have seen the animal or if they noticed anyone around your house who might have taken the pet or into whose vehicle the animal might have crawled and been accidentally taken away. They may also help to post handbills with the animal's picture or help you write an ad for the Lost and Found section of your local paper.

All that we have said about being honest with your children, helping them deal with possible guilt, and giving them permission to grieve at the death of an animal is also applicable here. You should certainly do all you can to recover your lost pet, but at some point, you and your children must move on if your pet is not recovered.

REHOMING

Even if you have made a real effort to acquire a pet at the right time and to select an animal that fits well in your family, circumstances do sometimes arise that mean finding another home is the best alternative for the animal and for you and your children. Such instances should be rare, but they do occur. Here we consider what some of them are and how best to handle them.

If you are rehoming a well-adjusted pet because of an unexpected change in your family circumstances or a family member's development of allergies that cannot be dealt with medically without relinquishing the animal, you should be able to find another suitable home for the animal. Your children will benefit from witnessing your taking responsibility for locating a good home for their pet and, if choices are available, may derive some comfort from being involved in the selection of their pet's new family.

Simply taking an animal to a shelter that kills those that are not adopted within a specific time and telling your children that it certainly found another loving family is dishonest. In all likelihood, they will later learn the truth and discern what may have happened to their pet. It may require a bit more effort and time, but you should be able to place an adoptable pet directly with a family or through an animal welfare organization that will ensure its placement in a suitable home.

Behavior problems are another reason that animals are relinquished. If such is the case with your pet, seriously consider whether you have done all you can to moderate the animal's behavior and whether it actually represents a danger to members of your household. Most animal behaviors that are simply annoying can be changed. Your veterinarian can provide you with practical tips for dealing with them or refer you to an obedience instructor or certified animal behaviorist.

If your animal is dangerous and, based on consultation with your veterinarian, you determine that there is little hope of moderating its behavior or of doing so without endangering members of your household or the community, euthanasia may be the most responsible alternative. In this case also, it is best to be honest with your children about what will happen to the animal. Children may well be attached even to a pet that proves to be dangerous and should be given permission to grieve just as they would for any other animal.

Pets should never be relinquished, nor should relinquishment be threatened, as a means of punishing a child. Parents often prohibit access to or take away a child's favorite "thing" as a means of punishment. We've all been on the commanding or receiving end of having TV privileges or special toys taken away because an infraction has been committed. Pets are often a child's favorite "thing." But taking away the pet teaches children that living animals are nothing more than possessions.

However necessary it is to relinquish a pet, parents must recognize that their children will grieve for the lost animal. Being forced to give up a companion animal is a major developmental event for children and its significance should not be underestimated.[3]

BEGINNING AGAIN

Parents are often tempted to immediately "replace" an animal that has died or been lost, thinking that this will ease the pain that their children are experiencing. This is usually a mistake. When the time is right to acquire another pet, both you and your child will know it.

Animals are unique living beings and one cannot replace another. Bringing another pet into the family prematurely is not fair to either the child or the new pet. Children may well feel disloyal to the memory of their lost pet if they accept a new one too quickly. They will gain more in the long run from moving through the experience of loss and be better prepared to accept a new pet later on. This may be true of parents as well.

We believe that a pet holds a special place in our hearts and cannot be replaced; however, people that love animals have big hearts that hold many special places. The new pet will find a place all his own.

CHAPTER SUMMARY

Points to Remember

- Parents should be honest with children about the actual or anticipated death of a pet or a pet's loss through theft or disappearance.
- Very young children (younger than age five) will not understand the meaning and finality of death.
- Parents should allow children to grieve the loss of their animal.
- Children will usually gain comfort from participating in rituals commemorating or mourning the loss of their pet.
- Parents should be sensitive to situations in which children may feel guilt related to the death or other loss of an animal and address this issue directly.
- Rehoming of a pet should be done only if absolutely necessary and every effort should be made to place an adoptable animal in a suitable home or with an organization or shelter that does so.
- Euthanasia should be considered for animals that are dangerously aggressive and whose behavior cannot be moderated or safely controlled.
- It is usually best to wait a while before acquiring a new pet after one dies or is lost.

Notes

INTRODUCTION

1. AVMA (American Veterinary Medical Association), Reference, Market Research Statistics, U.S. Pet Ownership—2007, www.avma.org/reference/marketstats/ownership.asp.

2. Judith M. Siegel, "Pet Ownership and the Importance of Pets among Adolescents," *Anthrozoös* 8, no. 4 (1995): 217–23; Vlasta V. Vidovic, Vesna V. Stetic, and Denis Bratko, "Pet Ownership, Type of Pet, and Socio-emotional Development of School Children," *Anthrozoös* 12, no. 4 (1999): 211–17.

3. National Council on Pet Population Study and Policy, Shelter Statistics Survey, 1994–97, www.petpopulation.org/statsurvey.html.

4. American Humane, Animal Shelter Euthanasia, www.americanhumane.org/site/PageServer?pagename=nr_fact_sheets_animal_euthanasia.

5. National Council on Pet Population Study and Policy, Exploring the Surplus Cat and Dog Problem: Highlights of Five Research Publications Regarding Relinquishment of Pets, www.petpopulation.org/exploring.pdf.

6. L. Neidhart and R. Boyd, "Companion Animal Adoption Study," *Journal of Applied Animal Welfare Science* 5, no. 3 (2002): 175–92.

CHAPTER 1

1. L. Ruggles and S. Hrncir, Preparing Fido, http://preparingfido.com/. The CD includes a selection of different baby sounds.

2. J. J. Sacks, M. Kresnow, and B. Houston, "Dog Bites: How Big a Problem?" *Injury Prevention* 2, no. 1 (1996): 52–54.

3. H. B. Weiss, D. I. Friedman, and J. H. Coben, "Incidence of Dog Bite Injuries Treated in Emergency Departments," *JAMA* 279, no. 1 (Jan. 7, 1998): 51–53.

CHAPTER 2

1. AVMA (American Veterinary Medical Association), Reference, Market Research Statistics, U.S. Pet Ownership—2007, www.avma.org/reference/marketstats/ownership.asp; Gail Melson, *Why the Wild Things Are: Animals in the Lives of Children* (Cambridge: Harvard University Press, 2001), 34.

2. Nienke Endenburg and Ben Baarda, "The Role of Pets in Enhancing Human Well-Being: Effects on Child Development," www.deltasociety.org/AnimalsHealthChildrenEnhancing.htm.

Reprinted from *The Waltham Book of Human-Animal Interactions: Benefits and Responsibilities [of Pet Ownership]* [New York: Pergamon, 1995].

3. Gail Melson, "Child Development and the Human–Companion Animal Bond," *American Behavioral Scientist* 47, no. 1 (2003): 31–39, 32.

4. Mary Renck Jalongo, ed., *The World's Children and Their Companion Animals: Developmental and Educational Significance of the Child/Pet Bond* (Olney, Md.: Association for Childhood Education International, 2004), 18.

5. M. J. Checchi, *Are You the Pet for Me? Choosing the Right Pet for Your Family* (New York: St. Martin's Press, 1999); Melson, *Why the Wild Things Are.*

6. Jalongo, *The World's Children and Their Companion Animals*; Jalongo cites Boris Levinson, *Pets and Human Development* (Springfield, Ill.:Thomas Publishing, 1972).

7. Aline H. Kidd and Robert M. Kidd, "Reactions of Infants and Toddlers to Live and Toy Animals," *Psychological Reports*, 61 (1987): 455–64.

8. Melson, "Child Development and the Human–Companion Animal Bond."

9. Elizabeth S. Paul, "Love of Pets and Love of People," in *Companion Animals and Us: Exploring the Relationship between People and Pets*, ed. Anthony L. Podberscek, Elizabeth S. Paul, and James A. Serpell (Cambridge, UK: Cambridge University Press, 2000); Paul cites studies by Poresky and Hendrix, 1990; Paul and Serpell, 1993; and Poresky, 1996.

10. Zuzanna Toeplitz, Anna Matczak, Anna Piotrowska, and Aleksandra Zygier, "Impact of Keeping Pets at Home upon the Social Development of Children," abstract, www.deltasociety.org/AnimalsHealthChildrenImpact.htm.

Paper presented at the Seventh International Conference on Human-Animal Interactions, Animals, Health, and Quality of Life, Sept., 6–9, 1995, Geneva, Switzerland.

11. Jalongo, *The World's Children and Their Companion Animals*; Jalongo cites L. Arambasic and G. Kerestes, "The Role of Pet Ownership as a Possible Buffer in Traumatic Experience," paper presented at the Eighth International Conference on Human-Animal Interactions, Prague, Czechoslovakia, Sept. 1998.

12. Melson, *Why the Wild Things Are*, 46; Melson cites Brenda K. Bryant, "Relevance of Pets and Neighborhood Animals to the Social-Emotional Functioning and Development of School-Age Children," Final Report to the Delta Society, Renton, Wash., 1986.

13. Beth A. Van Houtte and Patricia Jarvis, "The Role of Pets in Preadolescent Psychosocial Development," *Journal of Applied Developmental Psychology* 16, no. 3 (2002).

14. Aline H. Kidd and Robert M. Kidd, "Factors in Children's Attitudes toward Companion Animals," *Psychological Reports* 66 (1990): 775–86.

15. Melson, *Why the Wild Things Are*, 57.

16. Ibid, 58.

17. Brenda K. Bryant, "The Richness of the Child-Pet Relationship: A Consideration of Both Benefits and Costs of Pets to Children," *Anthrozoös* 3, no. 4 (1990): 253–61.

18. Jalongo, *The World's Children and Their Companion Animals*, 23, citing Melson, *Why the Wild Things*, and Carol D. Raupp, "Treasuring, Trashing, or Terrorizing: Adult Outcomes of Childhood

Socialization about Companion Animals" *Society and Animals* 7, no. 2 (1999): 141–49. Raupp reports research findings concerning the effects of parents' threatening to give children's pets away.

19. Aline H. Kidd and Robert M. Kidd, "Children's Drawings and Attachment to Pets," *Psychological Reports* 77, no. 1 (1995): 235–41.

20. Melson, "Child Development and the Human–Companion Animal Bond," 34–35; Melson cites Brenda K. Bryant, "The Neighborhood Walk: Sources of Support in Middle Childhood," *Monographs of the Society for Research in Child Development* 50, no. 3 (1986).

21. Bryant, "The Richness of the Child-Pet Relationship"; the quote is from Jalongo, *The World's Children and Their Companion Animals*, 29, citing C. Ross and J. Baron-Sorenson, *Pet Loss and Human Emotion: Guiding Clients through Grief* (Philadelphia: Accelerated Development, 1998).

22. Melson, *Why the Wild Things Are*, 34; Melson cites Michael Robin, Robert ten Bensel, Joseph S. Quigley, and Robert Anderson, "Childhood Pets and the Psychosocial Development of Adolescents," in *New Perspectives on Our lives with Companion Animals*, ed. Aaron H. Katcher and Alan M. Beck, 436–48 (Philadelphia: University of Pennsylvania Press, 1983).

23. Melson, *Why the Wild Things Are*, 36.

24. Judith, M. Siegel, "Pet Ownership and the Importance of Pets among Adolescents," *Anthrozoös* 8, no. 4 (1995): 217–23.

25. Aline H. Kidd and Robert M. Kidd, "Factors in Adult Attitudes toward Pets," *Psychological Reports* 65 (1989): 903–10; Elizabeth S. Paul and James A. Serpell, "Why Children Keep Pets: The Influence of Child and Family Characteristics," *Anthrozoös* 5, no. 4 (1992): 231–44.

26. L. Neidhart and R. Boyd, "Companion Animal Adoption Study," *Journal of Applied Animal Welfare Science* 5, no. 3 (2002): 175–92.

27. Kris Bulcroft, "Companion Animals in the American Family," *People, Animals, Environment* 8, no. 4 (1990): 13–14.

28. Paul and Serpell, "Why Children Keep Pets."

29. National Council on Pet Population Study and Policy, Exploring the Surplus Cat and Dog Problem: Highlights of Five Research Publications Regarding Relinquishment of Pets, www.petpopulation.org/exploring.pdf.

30. Ibid.

31. Jalongo, *The World's Children and Their Companion Animals;* Jalongo cites J. Goodall and M. Beckoff, *The Ten Trusts: What We Must Do to Care for the Animals We Love* (New York: Harper-Collins, 2003).

32. Melson, *Why the Wild Things Are.*

33. Jalongo, The World's Children and Their Companion Animals; Jalongo cites M. Salzman, "Pet Trends," *Vital Speeches of the Day* 67, no. 5 (2000): 147–53.

34. M. D. Salman, John G., New, Jr., Janet M. Scarlett, and Philip H. Kris, "Human and Animal Factors Related to the Relinquishment of Dogs and Cats in 12 Selected Animal Shelters in the United States," *Journal of Applied Animal Welfare Science* J, no. 3 (1998): 207–26.

35. National Council on Pet Population Study and Policy, Exploring the Surplus Cat and Dog Problem, www.petpopulation.org/exploring.pdf.

36. M. D. Salman, J. G. New Jr., J. M. Scarlett, P. H. Kass, R. Ruch-Gallie, and S. Hetts, "Human and Animal Factors Related to the Relinquishment of Dogs and Cats in Twelve Selected Animal Shelters in the United States," *Journal of Applied Animal Welfare Science* 1 no. 3 (July 1998): 207–26.

37. Jalongo, *The World's Children and Their Companion Animals,* 49; Jalongo cites a study conducted by Britain's Royal Society for the Prevention of Cruelty to Animals; findings are translated into U.S. currency.

CHAPTER 3

1. Monks of New Skete, *How to Be Your Dog's Best Friend: A Training Manual for Dog Owners* (Boston: Little, Brown, 1978); Monks of New Skete, *The Art of Raising a Puppy* (Boston: Little, Brown, 1991).

2. H. B. Weiss, D. I. Friedman, and J. H. Doben, "Incidence of Dog Bite Injuries Treated in Emergency Departments," *JAMA* 279 no. 1 (Jan. 7, 1998): 53, citing U.S. Consumer Product Safety Commission.

3. Dog Bite Statistics, compiled by Richard H. Polsky, www.dogexpert.com/Dog%20 Bite%20Statistics/DogBiteStatistics.html.

4. Dog Bite Law, Statistics, www.dogbitelaw.com/PAGES/statistics.html.

5. U.S. Centers for Disease Control, J. Gilchrist, Division of Unintentional Injury Prevention; K. Gotsch, J. L. Annest, and G. Ryan, Office of Statistics and Programming, National Center for Injury Prevention and Control.

6. Clifton Merritt, "Dog Attack Deaths and Maimings, U.S. and Canada, September 1982 to November 13," compiled by the editor of *Animal People,* www.dogbitelaw.com/Dog%20 Attacks%201982%20to%202006%20Clifton.pdf.

7. U.S. Centers for Disease Control, Nonfatal Dog Bites—Related Injuries Treated in Hospital Emergency Departments—United States, 2001,
www.cdc.gov/MMWR/preview/mmwrhtml/mm5226a1.htm.

8. Brenda K. Bryant, "The Richness of the Child-Pet Relationship: A Consideration of Both Benefits and Costs of Pets to Children," *Anthrozoös* 3, no. 4 (1990): 253–61; Vlasta V. Vidovic, Vesna V. Stetic, and Denis Bratko, "Pet Ownership, Type of Pet, and Socio-Emotional Development of School Children," *Anthrozoös* 12, no. 4 (1999): 211–17.

CHAPTER 5

1. Gail Melson, *Why the Wild Things Are: Animals in the Lives of Children* (Cambridge: Harvard University Press 2001); Melson cites J. Filiatre, J. Millot, and H. Montagner, "New Findings on Communication Behaviour between the Young Child and His Pet Dog," *Human-Pet Relationship* (1985): 50–57.

2. Mary Renck Jalongo, ed., *The Worlds' Children and Their Companion Animals: Developmental and Educational Significance of the Child/Pet Bond* (Olney, Md.: Association for Childhood

Education International, 2004); Jalongo cites Boris Levinson, *Companion Animals and Human Development* (Springfield, Ill.: Charles C. Thomas, 1972).

3. Jalongo, *The World's Children and Their Companion Animals.*

4. Melson, *Why the Wild Things Are.*

5. Elizabeth S. Paul and James A. Serpell, "Why Children Keep Pets: The Influence of Child and Family Characteristics," *Anthrozoös* 5, no. 4 (1992): 231–44.

6. Melson, *Why the Wild Things Are,* 48.

7. Virginia Morrow, "My Animals and Other Family: Children's Perspectives on their Relationships with Companion Animals," *Anthrozoös* 11, no. 4 (1998): 218–25.

8. Paul and Serpell, "Why Children Keep Pets"; Aline H. Kidd and Robert M. Kidd, "Factors in Children's Attitudes toward Companion Animals," *Psychological Reports* 80 (1990): 775–86.

9. ASPCA (American Society for the Prevention of Cruelty to Animals), Animal Behavior Center: Dog Behavior, A Guide to the Canine Behavior Professions, www.aspca.org/site/PageServer?pagename=pets_infoplease.

10. U.S. Centers for Disease Control, Nonfatal Dog Bites–Related Injuries Treated in Hospital Emergency Departments—United States, 2001,
   www.cdc.gov/MMWR/preview/mmwrhtml/mm5226a1.htm.

11. Jalongo *The World's Children and Their Companion Animals,* 74.

12. ASPCA, Animal Behavior Center: Dog Behavior, www.aspca.org/site/PageServer?pagename=pets_infoplease.

13. Child Welfare League of America National Data Analysis System, http://ndas.cwla.org/.

14. Rachael Harker, Glyn Collis, and June McNicholas, "The Influence of Current Relationships upon Pet Animal Acquisition," in *Companion Animals and Us,* ed. Anthony Podberscek, Elizabeth Paul, and James Serpell (Cambridge, UK: Cambridge University Press, 2000).

15. Frank Ascione, "Animal Abuse and Youth Violence," *Juvenile Justice Bulletin* (Sept. 2001), www.ncjrs.gov/html/ojjdp/jjbul2001_9_2/contents.html.

16. Growing Up with Pets, A Parent's Resource for Raising Happy Kids with Healthy Pets, www.growingupwithpets.com/index2.shtml.

CHAPTER 6

1. CDC, Parasitic Disease Information, Guidelines for Veterinarians, Prevention of Zoonotic Transmission of Ascarids and Hookworms of Dogs and Cats,
   www.cdc.gov/ncidod/dpd/parasites/ascaris/prevention.htm.

2. K. Won, D. Kruszon-Moran, P. Schantz, J. Jones. "National Seroprevalence and Risk Factors for Zoonotic *Toxocara* spp. Infection." Abstracts of the 56th American Society of Tropical Medicine and Hygiene. Philadelphia, Nov 4–8, 2007.

3. Peter M Schantz, and Jeanette K Stehr-Green, Division of Parasitic Diseases, Center for Infectious Diseases, CDC, Atlanta, Ga., Jan.1, 1988; reviewed 1995.

4. B. L. Blagburn, D. S. Lindsey, J. L. Vaughan, et al., "Prevalence of Canine Parasites Based on Fecal Flotation," *Compendium on Continuing Education for the Practicing Veterinarian* 18, no. 5 (1996): 483–509.

5. M. S. Perzanowski, E. Rönmark, T. A. E. Platts-Mills, and B. Lundbäck, "Effect of Cat and Dog Ownership on Sensitization and Development of Asthma among Preteenage Children," *American Journal of Respiratory Critical Care Medicine* 166 (2002): 696–702.

6. D. Oberle, E. von Mutius, and R. von Kries, "Childhood Asthma and Continuous Exposure to Cats since the First Year of Life with Cats Allowed in the Child's Bedroom, *Allergy* 58, no. 10 (Oct. 2003): 1033–36.

7. C. Almqvist, A. C. Egmar, G. Hedlin, M. Lundqvist, S. L. Nordvalls, G. Pershagen, M. Svartengren, M. Hage-Hamsten, and M. Wickman, "Direct and Indirect Exposure to Pets— Risk of Sensitization and Asthma at Four Years in a Birth Cohort," *Clinical and Experimental Allergy* 33, no. 9 (Sept. 2003): 1190–97.

8. Leonard B. Bacharier and Robert C. Strunk, "Pets and Childhood Asthma—How Should the Pediatrician Respond to New Information That Pets May Prevent Asthma?" *Pediatrics* 112, no. 4 (Oct. 2003): 974–76.

9. C. G. Bornehag, L. Sundell, L. Hagerhed, S. Janson, and the DBH Study Group, "Pet-Keeping in Early Childhood and Airway, Nose, and Skin Symptoms Later In Life," *Allergy* 58, no. 9 (Sept. 2003): 939–44.

10. S. A. Plotkin, "Rabies," *Clinical Infectious Diseases* 30 (2000): 4–12.

CHAPTER 7

1. Gail Melson, *Why the Wild Things Are: Animals in the Lives of Children* (Cambridge: Harvard University Press, 2001).

2. Ibid.

3. Ibid.; Carol D. Raupp, "Treasuring, Trashing, or Terrorizing: Adult Outcomes of Childhood Socialization about Companion Animals," *Society and Animals* 7, no. 2 (1999): 141–59.

Index

accommodations for pets: doghouses and kennels, 60, 81–82; fencing, 60–61, 80–81; indoor accommodations, 61–62, 82; outdoor accommodations, 37–38, 59–60; retreat spaces, 61, 98

adolescents, and pets, 101–2, 107–8

adopting a pet, 46, 52; adult pets, 52

allergies, and pets, 125; allergy studies, 125–27

American College of Veterinary Behaviorists, 105

American Medical Association (AMA), 129

American Veterinary Medical Association (AVMA), 31

animal abuse, 110

Animal Behavior Society, 105

animal neglect, 38, 109

animal shelters, 2; numbers of animals in, 2; reasons for relinquishment of pets to, 2, 37, 38–40, 137–38

Association of Companion Animal Behavior Counselors, 105

babies, and pets, 8–9, 32–33, 99; after-baby checklist, 28–29; before-baby checklist (first, second, and third trimesters), 28; desensitizing pets to baby food and formula, 16–17; desensitizing pets to baby lotions, powders, and the like, 15–16; desensitizing pets to baby-related noises, 12–14; desensitizing pets to diapers, 14–15; first introduction of the baby to the pet, 23–24; including pets in baby care, 26; introducing pets to baby paraphernalia, 10–12; keeping pets out of nurseries and babies' beds, 19–21; supervision of (the "unbreakable rule"), 24–26; and toy-sharing, 17–19

bathing pets. *See* grooming pets: bathing

behavior management: and behavior specialists, 104–5; and cats, 17, 20–21, 103–4; and dogs, 102–3; praise, 11–12, 17, 14; reprimands, 11–12, 17; and toy-sharing, 18; and treats, 14. *See also* obedience training

birds, 62

breeding pets, 39, 111–12

cat scratch fever (*Bartonella henselae* infection), 124

cats: avoidance of children, 51; and babies, 12, 15, 19–21; and baby formula, 16; bathing of, 90–92; and behavior management, 17, 20–21, 103–4; brushing of, 90; and the clawing of furniture, 104; declawing of, 104; eating of baby wipes, 16; exercising of, 79; feeding of, 70, 71, 74; immunizations for, 87; injuries caused by, 26, 59, 104; life expectancy of, 52; and litter boxes, 20, 76–77; myths about "stealing cats *(continued)*

baby's breath," 19; outside cats, 81, 82; professional grooming of, 53, 92–93; reasons for keeping a cat indoors, 81, 82; and safe spaces, 51, 98, 100; and scratching, 104; size of, 51; and spraying, 21; and urinary infections and blockages, 77

Centers for Disease Control (CDC), 25, 118

Certification Council for Professional Dog Trainers (CPDT), 102

childless couples, and pets, 7–8

children, and pets, 100–101; attachment of children to pets, 35; child-pet interaction checklist, 113; and the development of care-giving roles in children, 34; encounters with pets outside the home, 110–11; factors affecting child-pet interactions, 97; and Grandma's Law bargaining, 109; importance of pets in children's physical and mental development, 32–33; importance of pets in children's psychosocial development, 33; importance of pets in children's social development, 32; importance of pets in the development of empathy and compassion, 33; and the loss of a pet, 35, 36, 134–38; and parental supervision, 97–98, 99, 100; and pet-care chores, 72–73, 106–7, 108–9

choosing a pet, issues to consider when: accommodations (outside and inside), 59–62; age (of the pet), 51–53; appearance/breed, 53–54; early socialization, 52, 57–58; exercise requirements, 55–56, 60; exotic or alternative pets, 62–63; physical health, 64; price, 46; selecting the right pet checklist, 67; size, 50–51; temperament, 56–57, 58; veterinary input, 63, 64–65

Companion Animal Parasite Council (CAPC), 121, 129; Web site of, 131

death of pets. *See* pet loss: through death

diseases. *See specific diseases*

dog bites, 12, 25, 58–59, 103; breeds that are prone to bite, 59; prevalence of, among children, 58–59

dog parks, 78–79

dogs: aggression in, 79; and babies, 12; bathing of, 90–92; and behavior management (*see* obedience training); big dogs, 50; brachycephalic breeds, 54; brushing of, 90; and crates, 98, 100; eating of baby wipes, 16; eating of diaper contents, 14–15; exercising of, 55–56, 77–79; feeding of, 70, 71; housebreaking of, 74–76; immunizations for, 87; and latrine duty, 74–76; life expectancy of, 52; little dogs, 51; midsize dogs, 51; outside accommodations for, 59–61; and pack mentality, 8, 12, 38, 103; professional grooming of, 53–54, 92–93; size of, 50–51; temperament of, 57–58. *See also* dog bites; dog parks

euthanasia, 135–36

exotic (alternative) pets, 62–63; injuries caused by, 62. *See also* birds; ferrets; rabbits

feeding pets, 65; changing diets (food conversion), 70; as a child's chore/responsibility, 72–73, 108–9; choosing the right food, 69–70; cost of, 48; the feeding area, 73–74; feeding schedules, 71–72; food bowls, 73; and food quality, 71; monitoring food intake, 74; and "people food," 71; treats, 72; water, 72–73, 74

ferrets, 62

grooming pets, 53–54, 90–93; bathing,

90–92; brushing, 90; professional grooming, 53, 54, 92

"Growing Up with Pets" Web site, 131

heartworms, 121; human heartworm infection, 122; prevention of, in dogs and cats, 122–23; transmission of, 121–22

hookworms, 119–20; prevention of, 120–21; transmission of, 119

Levinson, Boris, 32, 99

Lyme disease (*Borrelia burgdorferi* infection), 127

mange (scabies), 124; human mange infection, 125

MRSA (methicillin-resistant Staphylococcus aureus) infection, 128–29

multiple-pet households, 47

neutering (castration), 47–48, 87. *See also* spaying (ovariohysterectomy)

obedience training, 9–10, 48, 102–3; and professional trainers, 102; and voice commands, 9–10, 78

parasites. *See* hookworms; roundworms (*Toxocara canis, Toxocara cati*)

pet care, 106–7; cost of, 40, 48–49, 53–54, 60, 61; and household schedules and routines, 8, 26; managing change, 107–8. *See also* feeding pets; grooming pets; veterinary care

pet loss: and children, 35, 36, 134–38; replacing a lost pet, 138–39; through death, 35, 36, 133–36; through relinquishment (*see* relinquishing pets); through theft or disappearance, 137

pet loss prevention: commonsense precautions, 84–85; identification tags, 83; microchipping, 83–84

pet ownership: benefits of, 8; and health risks, 129; rates and prevalence of in the West, 31, 36; sources of information about, 39

pet readiness issues: accommodations for a pet, 37–38; the cost of pet maintenance, 40, 48–49, 53–54, 60, 61; family relationships, 38; future family plans, 39–40; lack of information on pets' needs and behaviors, 38–39; parents' attitudes toward pet ownership, 37; pet readiness checklist, 41–42

potential health risks checklist, 130

"Preparing Fido" CD (Lisa Ruggles and Shawn Hrncir), 13

preschoolers, and pets, 34, 100, 107

rabbits, 62, 111

rabies, 128

rehoming pets, 137–38. *See also* relinquishing pets

relinquishing pets, 2, 137–38; and children, 35, 36; reasons for, 2, 37, 38–39, 40, 137–38

ringworm, 123

roundworms (*Toxocara canis, Toxocara cati*): human roundworm infection (larval migrans), 117–18; incidence of roundworm infection in humans, 118–19; prevention of, 120–21; transmission of, 116

shedding, 53, 93; myths concerning, 53

sleeping arrangements, and pets, 21–22, 61

spaying (ovariohysterectomy), 47–48, 87

strays, 46–47

tick-borne diseases, 127. *See also* Lyme disease (*Borrelia burgdorferi* infection)